Marilyn Lake, Henry Reynolds, Mark M  winning historians of twentieth century Australia. Lead authors Marilyn Lake and Henry Reynolds recently co-authored *Drawing the Global Colour Line: White Men's Countries and the Question of Racial Equality* which won the Queensland Premier's Prize for History and the Ernest Scott Prize, and were joint winners of the Prime Minister's Prize for Non-Fiction.

MARILYN LAKE is professor of history at La Trobe University. She is the author and co-author of a number of books including *The Limits of Hope: Soldier Settlement in Victoria 1915–38*; *Creating a Nation* (co-author); the biography, *FAITH: Faith Bandler, Gentle Activist* and *Getting Equal: The History of Feminism in Australia*.

HENRY REYNOLDS is professor of history at the University of Tasmania and is author of many books including *The Other Side of the Frontier: Aboriginal Resistance to the European Invasion of Australia*; *Frontier: Aborigines, Settlers and Land*; *Why Weren't We Told? A Personal Search for the Truth About Our History* and *Nowhere People*.

MARK MCKENNA is associate professor at the University of Sydney. He is the author of *This Country: A Reconciled Republic?*; *Looking for Blackfellas' Point: An Australian History of Place*; *The Captive Republic: A History of Republicanism in Australia, 1788–1996* and co-editor of *Australian Republicanism: A Reader*. His biography of Manning Clark will be published this year.

JOY DAMOUSI is professor of history at the University of Melbourne. She is the author of *Depraved and Disorderly: Female Convicts, Sexuality and Gender in Colonial Australia*; *The Labour of Loss: Mourning, Memory and Wartime Bereavement in Australia*; *Freud in the Antipodes: A Cultural History of Psychoanalysis in Australia* and co-author of *Footy Passions*.

CARINA DONALDSON is a postgraduate student in history at La Trobe University. She is writing a PhD thesis on the memorialisation of the Vietnam War.

WHAT'S WRONG WITH ANZAC?

THE MILITARISATION OF AUSTRALIAN HISTORY

Marilyn Lake and Henry Reynolds

with Mark McKenna and Joy Damousi

NEW
SOUTH

A New South book

Published by
University of New South Wales Press Ltd
University of New South Wales
Sydney NSW 2052
AUSTRALIA
www.unswpress.com.au

© Marilyn Lake, Henry Reynolds, Mark McKenna and Joy Damousi 2010
First published 2010

10 9 8 7 6 5 4 3 2

National Library of Australia
Cataloguing-in-Publication entry
        Title: What's wrong with Anzac?/Marilyn Lake ... [et. al.]
        Edition: 1st ed.
        ISBN: 978 1 74223 151 8 (pbk.)
        Notes: Includes index.
            Bibliography.
        Subjects: Australia. Army. Australian and New Zealand Army Corps.
            World War, 1914–1918 – Historiography.
            Collective memory.
            History – Psychological aspects.
            Australia – Historiography.
        Other Authors/Contributors: Lake, Marilyn.
        Dewey Number: 940.394072

Design Josephine Pajor-Markus
Cover Design by Committee
Cover image Getty Images
Printer Ligare

This book is printed on paper using fibre supplied from plantation or sustainably
managed forests.

CONTENTS

PREFACE

For several years now Australia has seen the relentless militarisation of our history: the commemoration of war and understandings of our national history have been confused and conflated. The Anzac spirit is now said to animate all our greatest achievements, even as the Anzac landing recedes into the distant past.

Anzac Day has been promoted as our national day, but there has been a resurgence, too, in Remembrance Day, VP Day and Vietnam Veterans' Day. Since 1990, when Bob Hawke became the first Australian prime minister to preside over the Dawn Service at Anzac Cove, we have witnessed an extraordinary increase in the number of books, newspaper articles, documentaries and electronic media programmes devoted to the history of Australians at war. Political leaders of all persuasions, government departments led by the Department of Veterans' Affairs, national institutions such as the Australian War Memorial, mass media, opinion makers, publishers and schools in every state and territory now either actively fund or promote the commemoration of Australians at war, whether at Gallipoli, Fromelles or Kokoda, in Korea and Vietnam, not just on special days, but throughout the year.

Yet the sudden rush to embrace 25 April as *the* Australian story has resulted in a crowning irony: in transforming Anzac Day into a sacred myth, we have forgotten our rich and diverse history of nation-making and distorted the history of Gallipoli and its Imperial context and consequences.

As Australian historians, we have written this book because we are deeply concerned about many aspects of the Anzac resurgence. We are concerned about the extraordinary government intervention in promoting Anzac Day, most of which has occurred without people knowing its true extent. We are also concerned about the misrepresentation and forgetting of our broader history.

History runs counter to myth-making. We write to encourage a more critical and truthful public debate about the uses of the Anzac myth. We write because we want to do justice to Australia's long anti-war tradition which was born in revulsion at the terrible cost of war. Most importantly we write because we think it is time to reclaim our national civil and political traditions of democratic equality and social justice in whose name we now ask our soldiers to fight.

NOTE Although the Australian and New Zealand Army Corps may be abbreviated as ANZAC we follow common usage in writing 'Anzac' in lower case, as in CEW Bean's 'The Anzac Book' and the designation of 25 April as Anzac Day.

INTRODUCTION
What have you done for your country?

Marilyn Lake

'My question is: what have you done for your country?
... please no lecturing. You haven't earned the right.'

Email to author, 23 April 2009

'Questioning the cultural primacy of the Anzac myth
is neither traitorous nor disrespectful of the dead.'

Potoroo, *Age* blog, 23 April 2009[1]

To write about what's wrong with Anzac today is to court the charge of treason. And much else besides. When I presented a public lecture on the subject last April, which was printed in an abridged version as an 'Opinion' piece in the *Age* newspaper, and later broadcast on Radio National, an avalanche of correspondence descended, much of it in the form of personal abuse and accusations of disloyalty. In the *Age* blog that followed emotions ran high.

I had been invited by the History Teachers' Association of Victoria and the University of Melbourne to give a lecture on the 'Myth of Anzac' in a series on 'Mythologies'. I addressed the power of Anzac mythology in Australia today and the way that it had come to serve as White Australia's creation myth.

Federation had inaugurated the Commonwealth of Australia as a new nation state in 1901, but clearly many felt that – at the symbolic level at least – that there was something missing.

It was at Gallipoli on 25 April 1915, so the legend ran, that the Australian and New Zealand Army Corps (ANZACs) made good: a nation was born on that day of death. War provided the supreme test of nationhood. As the official war historian, CEW Bean wrote, the Great War served as a test of Australian national character and the men of the Australian Imperial Force (AIF) had passed that test triumphantly. Despite the Gallipoli campaign ending months later in military defeat, for Australia its triumph lay in

> the mettle of the men themselves. To be the sort of man who would give way when his mates were trusting to his firmness … to live the rest of his life haunted by the knowledge that he had set his hand to a soldier's task and had lacked the grit to carry it through – that was the prospect which these men could not face. Life was very dear, but life was not worth living unless they could be true to their idea of Australian manhood.[2]

In proving their manhood – brave, firm, loyal and steadfast – these men (so it was said) had proven our nationhood.

But now in the twenty-first century, I suggested in the lecture, perhaps it was time to move on from such Imperial myths and proclaim ourselves a free and independent republic, enshrining not militarist values, but the civil and political values of equality and justice, which in an earlier era had been thought to define a distinctive 'Australian ethos'. At its heart was an 'egalitarian social doctrine', as leading historian Bob Gollan had written, 'a belief in equality of opportunity, and a conviction that in Australia men had a right to a good life'.[3] That aspiration was widely attractive to diverse Australians including Chinese colonists who joined in the celebration of Federation in 1901, as John Fitzgerald has noted, even though they were subject to systematic racial discrimination. From the 1870s Chinese Australians had invoked Australia's commitment to equality and common human rights to argue for their own citizen rights and for a multicultural Australia. Similarly early Aboriginal campaigns had demanded that political leaders extend the Australian principle of equality to grant full citizenship to Australia's Indigenous people.

It was time, I suggested in the lecture, for Australians to reclaim the best of our social and political traditions that had long defined the aspiration towards economic, social, sexual and racial equality as definitive of Australian values. This commitment to equality was reinforced when Australian women became the first in the world to win full political rights, possibly the only turning point in world history in which Australians led the way. Should not these distinctive national traditions and values inspire political leaders today, inform their public pronouncements and help shape national policy?

Anzac Day had in any case long since ceased to be a day of solemn remembrance and become a festive event, celebrated by backpackers wrapped in flags, playing rock music, drinking beer and proclaiming their national identity on the distant shores of Turkey. Surely it was inappropriate, I suggested in the lecture, for a modern democratic nation to adopt an Imperial, masculine, militarist event as the focus of our national self-definition in the twenty-first century.

What have you done for your country?

The responses to the lecture, newspaper article and radio broadcast were immediate and passionate. They contained a mixture of hostility and support, personal abuse and thoughtful reflection. Some indignant *Age* bloggers said that I had no right to write on this topic. What had academics and 'clever dick historians' – especially female ones – ever done for their country except show lack of patriotic pride? 'This fool of a woman should be charged with treason!!' fulminated one critic. His advice was forthright: 'Be quiet and be grateful.' To interrogate the myth of Anzac was un-Australian and disrespectful. 'How disgusting to call ANZAC a "myth"', added Rick. 'Get a reel job [sic].' To refer to Anzac as a 'myth' said another was 'unconscionable'. 'And she calls herself Australian?'

But there were as many contributors to the *Age* online forum and personal correspondents who expressed relief. 'It came as a bright light amidst all the Anzac fanfare', wrote one. 'Congratulations!' 'Australia needs to drop the sentimental garbage that ANZAC day has become', said another. 'The soldiers of Gallipoli must be honoured however they are not apostles to be given religious reverence.' 'The Anzac fixation was always a bit odd, but during the Howard years it went completely off the rails', wrote Neil. 'The annual backpacker festival at Gallipoli is flat-out weird. I'm confident the average attendee's knowledge of WW1 would comfortably fit on the back of a postage stamp.' And from another happy blogger: 'finally someone with the courage to stand up to the constant soldier worshipping we do here. Thank you, thank you, thank you!'

The Anzac spirit

For some correspondents, the significance of the 'Anzac spirit' went far beyond the commemoration of our war dead. Rather it gave meaning to all our history. It was the 'very lifeblood of the country', animating all national achievement:

> The ANZAC spirit, ethereal it may be, is the impetus behind our never say die attitude, the reason we excel at sport, the reason the country galvanized behind the victims of the Victorian bushfires, the reason we came to the aid of East Timor … ANZAC day is not just about honouring the war achievements and bravery of the war dead but acknowledging the virtues of our nation past and present so that they may be preserved for future generations.

These sentiments faithfully echo the message promoted by official organisers of Anzac Day rituals:

> The Spirit of ANZAC is an intangible thing. It is unseen, unpredictable, an unquestionable thirst for justice, freedom and peace … the spirit of ANZAC is a cornerstone which underpins our Australian image, way of life and indeed is an integral part of our heritage.[4]

But such rhapsodies received short shrift from more cynical contributors to the debate who pointed to different history lessons. The Anzacs 'were not the first from our nation to work with allied nations in stupid wars, and they are definitely not the last' wrote Groggo. 'The one thing that stands out in all the Anzac hooha is that you are basically celebrating a magnificent tactical ballsup (historical fact) engineered by our mates the poms why don't we get free of the poms and celebrate that?'

'Regarding Anzac', wrote Troy, 'We should be remembering people of peace not people of war. Anzac only reminds us of WAR. Australia has always been fighting someone else's war.' 'In past years ANZAC Day has changed from remembering the dead soldiers who sacrificed their lives fighting other countries' wars to glorifying war', suggested Frank. 'This type of glorification is making it easier for the world's politicians to go to war instead of using diplomacy to solve problems that crop up between countries.'

Central to the discussion was a dispute over the meaning of our engagement in foreign wars and their relevance to our national history and identity. Australians didn't die to defend their freedom, observed Marg, but always fought in the interests of other countries: 'Modern Australia was never in danger of being invaded by anyone ... Instead European Australians' forebears were the invaders of the First Australians' homeland.' 'Identity is layered and plural', Frankie suggested, 'and to suggest that we as a nation should define ourselves solely through war takes away from the variety of experiences of Australian history, not least of which is a war on Indigenous people that goes unacknowledged'.

Meanwhile, Daniel worried about the significance of the battle at Anzac Cove: 'Because I can't remember my high school history, could someone please tell me how crucial the battle of ANZAC cove was to the war? If "we" had lost there, would our lives today in Australia really be very different?' No wonder Prime Minister John Howard had called for 'a root and branch renewal of the teaching of Australian history in our schools'.[5]

That the Allied forces were defeated at Gallipoli – the landing being followed by the evacuation – meant of course that nationalist myth-making had to focus on a different sort of triumph, as official historian CEW Bean recognised, which was the demonstration of 'manly character' now known in more gender neutral terms as 'the spirit of Anzac'. As Murray described it online: 'Stand by your mates and never ever give up. Why would we ever want to forget that?' But was mateship really distinctive to Australians? 'What's this yammering about "mateship", as if it's a unique Aussie characteristic', asked Max. 'You think Russians, Americans, Chinese, French, Germans, Italians, Egyptians, Brazilians, Mongolians or anybody else don't have mates?'

The *Age* online forum on the Myth of Anzac attracted more than two hundred contributors to a lively, heated exchange that revealed not only deep divisions over the meaning of Anzac, but also how intertwined Australian history, identity and war commemoration have now become. In public mythologising, Gallipoli has become a sacred place, consecrated land, which the sovereign Turks disturb at their peril. Anzac Day is our national day, so the legend now asserts, because Australians fought there for our 'freedom and democracy' – even though the Anzacs landed at Gallipoli to assist our great ally and the world's greatest autocracy, Russia. The diggers did not invade Turkey to defend democracy.

Many contributors to the debate were aware that Australians enlisted in World War 1 to fight for king and empire. In fact a disproportionate number of the first recruits were English migrants. 'The hard facts of history' wrote Yakman to his fellow bloggers, 'tell us that the Dardanelles campaign was instigated by Churchill at the urging of the Czar of Russia to open up a new battle front at a time when Russia was being hammered by the Germans and there was a stalemate on the western front'.

Australians went to Gallipoli at the behest of the British,

to aid the Mother Country. They served the empire well, as the British war correspondent Ellis Ashmead-Bartlett affirmed in his report of the pleasing performance of the 'colonials' in April 1915:

> In less than a quarter of an hour the Turks were out of their second position, either bayoneted or fleeing ...
>
> But then the Australians, whose blood was up, instead of entrenching, rushed northwards and eastwards, searching for fresh enemies to bayonet ...
>
> These raw colonial troops in these desperate hours proved worthy to fight side by side with the heroes of Mons, the Aisne, Ypres and Neuve Chapelle.
>
> Early in the morning of April 26 the Turks repeatedly tried to drive the colonials from their position. The colonials made local counter-attacks, and drove off the enemy at the point of the bayonet, which the Turks would never face.[6]

The Turks were assumed to be cowards, but even so Ashmead-Bartlett was particularly impressed at the Anzacs' dazzling skill with the bayonet especially when their 'blood was up'.

Today the cause of the war has been largely forgotten and its Imperial dimension is ignored. Rather, a new story of our expeditionary forces fighting for freedom and democracy has taken hold and it has been extended to cover all twentieth century wars: 'our freedoms [were] defended by Australian service men and women in Gallipoli, WW2, Korea, Malaya, Vietnam, Iraq and Afghanistan' wrote Paul. To which Troy replied: 'Freedom, freedom, freedom! We sound like brainwashed Americans'. But Brett was drawn to the story of freedom and the soldier's role in securing it: 'It is the soldier, not the reporter who has given us freedom of the press. It is the soldier, not the protest organiser who has given us freedom of speech'.

When did the story of Anzacs fighting for our freedom begin? Certainly Americans have long told this story about their own history. 'No idea is more fundamental to Americans' sense of themselves as individuals and as a nation than freedom' wrote the US historian Eric Foner in *The Story of American Freedom* in 1998.[7] Indeed Barak Obama invoked this history in his Inauguration Address. But since when has the idea of fighting for freedom been central to the stories Australians tell about themselves? It was democratic equality and the fair go, the demand for justice and the assertion of rights that were once central to Australians' 'sense of themselves'. At the heart of Australian nationalism, was a belief in equality of opportunity, but 'equality of opportunity' is not a value invoked by the 'spirit of Anzac'. Even as its custodians do their very best to make it inclusive, welcoming Aborigines and women into the ranks of Anzacs, such efforts ironically testify to the depth of the traditional Australian commitment to equality.

Many participants in the online debate who felt uncomfortable with the myth-making attached to Anzac invoked the 'facts of history': 'We have never been independent and have always followed our colonial masters – whether UK or currently USA. All of our wars including WW2 were in fact due to our compliance with Pax Britania [sic] or Pax America. We have never gone to war for freedom or democracy as the marketing slogans perpetuate'. Michael told readers of the *Age* that he had only recently discovered that other countries had more troops in the Allied forces at Gallipoli than Australia: 'Turks, appx 80 000, Great Britain appx 30 000, French appx 12 000 … Australia appx 8500, NZ appx 3500'. Indeed the landing was an international affair, not a narrowly national one and is best understood as part of the larger history of an Imperial world in which empires came into deadly conflict.

Other contributors to the debate urged readers to remember that far from fighting for Australian freedom, Australians invaded Turkey in 1915, a country that in no way threatened Australia. Now in 2009 it was still their sovereign territory despite the regular invasion each April and Australian outrage at local road improvements. 'If anyone can show me how invading Turkey in 1915 was in any way a defence of our freedoms, I would love to hear about it. In what way were the Turks threatening our Australian way of life?' Or as JLT suggested: 'Let us not forget that the Anzacs were not defending Australia or our way of life, but were attacking and invading the Ottoman empire. If that is nation-building and defines Australia then we are defined by killing Turks defending their country.' This was a disconcerting thought. As Daniel noted: 'it's extremely difficult to understand where the facts end and the myths/legends begin concerning Anzac'.

In my public lecture I wanted to show that the mythologising of Anzac as our national creation story and the popular re-writing of history that had occurred as a result had effectively marginalised other formative experiences, especially cultural, social and political achievements in the making of the nation. I suggested that the militarisation of Australian history in schools – which had dramatically accelerated with the entry of the Department of Veterans' Affairs into the business of pedagogy and curriculum design – had worked to sideline different stories of nation-building, oriented not to military prowess, but to visions of social justice and democratic equality. Surely Australians who had fought for sexual and racial equality had contributed more significantly to securing our democratic freedoms?

We are now regularly told, however, by politicians, the media and the educationists at Department of Veterans' Affairs that our national values derive from the military values displayed in battle, usually listed as courage, mateship and sacrifice, but not aggression, conformity, obedience to orders and a capacity to kill people. 'It is about the celebration of some wonderful values', Prime Minister Howard said in his Anzac Address in Canberra in 2003, 'of courage, of valour, of mateship, of decency, of a willingness as a nation to do the right thing, whatever the cost'.

Such eulogies forget that soldiers don't just die for their country, they also kill for it, sometimes in murderous rampages and covert massacres as recent research on the Light Horse Brigade in Palestine has highlighted. Our soldiers have been involved in many wars – from Vietnam to Iraq – that have inflicted terrible deaths and injuries on hundreds of thousands of innocent civilians in villages, towns and countrysides. Whereas this 'collateral damage' was obvious in television coverage of the Vietnam War on the nightly news, we rarely see reports of civilian deaths and the destruction of villages in Afghanistan.

Overseas battlefields have now become key national sites for Australians, where, school students are told, Australian history really happened. 'You feel as an Australian', said Prime Minister Howard nominating Anzac Cove to head the National Heritage List, 'it's as much a part of Australia as the land on which your home is built'.[8] Many bloggers at the *Age* suggested that one only needed to go to Gallipoli to understand our history, to 'see what it means first hand'. 'I have been to Gallipoli myself', wrote Kim, 'and seen what our troops had to contend with'. He had seen 'the actual trenches'. Others had a rather more cynical take on the pilgrimage to battlefields: 'Bogans running around getting drunk at Gallipoli, our national identity'.

One visitor felt he had to explain to European tourists what Australians were celebrating. 'After answering several Europeans' questions on the subject of what it was all about, Basques, Dutch and Germans were stunned that a country would go to a place they invaded, visiting in such vast numbers in often flagrant nationalistic displays, whilst the invaded country profited by ripping them off on tours and selling them drinks. A quiet commemoration is one thing, but tens of thousands, many with little or no connection to the events, arriving en masse is another.'

During the last ten years, military history has become central to popular understandings of Australian history and in the process the rightful honouring of the war dead and the writing of national history have been conflated. Australian history has been thoroughly militarised. But because war commemoration centres on timeless military virtues – 'the Anzac spirit' – this new account of the national past is ironically profoundly ahistorical: all wars become one. History becomes a series of battles – at Gallipoli, the Somme, Fromelles, Kokoda, Tobruk, Long Tan, Oruzgan Province – in which the protagonists all demonstrate the same heroic virtues. Historical specificity, difference and changing contexts are lost sight of. For all the insistence of prime ministers Howard and Rudd on 'the facts of history' it is the 'facts' that get completely submerged in the mythology.

Rather all battlefields become sites in one continuous war with Australian soldiers cast as always 'fighting for our freedom', their service always serving to 'unite the nation'. 'What does it matter if we focus on a military disaster', wrote Pete, 'as long as it unites the nation'. 'To me Anzac day is so much more than Gallipoli', wrote Troy. 'It's France, Changi, the Kokoda trail, the army nurses who lost their lives during the fall of Singapore and those who suffered at the hands of the Japanese.' Indeed in a recent book by Peter Rees nurses at war have been paid the ultimate honour as *The Other Anzacs*.

That World War 1 and Vietnam were in fact unpopular wars that deeply divided the nation does not sit easily with the myth of nation-building. 'The focus on the Gallipoli campaign to the detriment of other significant historical events can be a problem', wrote Peter, 'I would argue that the rejection of the referenda for conscription in 1916 and 1917 was also fairly significant, but it was divisive rather than unifying so it rarely gets a look in'. Many Australians know, of course, from family experience that participation in the wars could be a devastating and deeply demoralising experience. 'My great grandfather served in Fromelles', wrote Troy. 'Luckily he lived to be 101 and I experienced his stories and views first hand. He refused to attend an Anzac day ceremony and … let me assure you, he would be turning in his grave if he could see what ANZAC day had now become. At the time, like many ANZACS he was an unworldly and naïve young man, voluntarily enlisting in the meat grinder and his actions were mostly driven by primordial instincts, not some collective and god like 'Australian' courage.'

As we show in chapter three, World War 1 and Vietnam generated strong anti-war movements, which called into question the purpose and legitimacy of those wars. The large peace movements that resulted are now largely lost to memory. Anti-war protesters in the 1960s and 1970s are now depicted as 'anti-Anzac'. 'Australian troops returning from Vietnam were spat on courtesy of Jim Cairns and the media' wrote Woody in the online debate. But another blogger took issue with this story. Was this simply a new myth in the making that if repeated often enough would become a truth? 'Care to offer any evidence that returning Australian soldiers were actually spat upon by Jim Cairns – or anybody else for that matter?' asked Redsaunas. 'Yet another myth to add to the mountain of soldier worship myths this country groans under.'

To be accused of being 'anti-Anzac' in Australia today is to be charged with the most grievous offence. 'I find your article deeply insulting and offensive', wrote one blogger. 'You can't rewrite history, sorry. You are a revisionist.' But who is re-writing Australian history? There are now more books published on Australians at war than ever before, hundreds during the last two decades alone. The shelves of bookshops groan under their weight and military history is usually given its own section of the shop. The myth of Anzac now dominates our understanding of Australian history and national identity, but it wasn't always so. This shift in values is in need of explanation.

It is not the case as many now assume that earlier historians saw the landing at Gallipoli as 'a seminal moment in modern Australian history' as one blogger suggested. Indeed it would come as a shock to many to realise that past histories of Australia, even officially sponsored ones, could omit all reference to Anzac and Gallipoli. Gordon Greenwood's widely read text, *Australia: A Social and Political History*, officially sponsored by the Arts Sub-Committee of the 1951 Jubilee Celebrations Committee of the Commonwealth of Australia, first published in 1955 and reprinted many times in the 1960s and 1970s, has, astonishingly, no index entry to ANZAC, Anzac Day, Gallipoli, CEW Bean or the Returned Services League (RSL).

In 1964 a survey of Australian historiography in the *Pattern of Australian Culture* omitted any reference to CEW Bean and the story of Anzac.[9] As historian Ken Inglis told a gathering of his colleagues in Canberra that year, Australian historians, caught up in the political romance of the defeat of the conscription referenda, took no interest in the war itself. He thought that it was time they did and would soon recruit a bright young PhD student, Bill Gammage, who followed the example of CEW Bean, in rendering the experience of ordinary soldiers central to the history of World War 1.[10]

Throughout most of the twentieth century, the commemoration of the war dead on Anzac Day and the writing of Australian history had proceeded as quite separate and unrelated activities. Certainly Bean's idea that 'the consciousness of Australian nationhood was born at Gallipoli' had become the 'liturgy of Anzac Day', as historian Geoff Serle remarked, but not the stuff of national history.[11] Historians tended to pursue social and political themes and they found the emergence of a sense of Australian nationhood – an Australian ethos – elsewhere in the romance of the bush or nationalist literature, in the vision of the Heidelberg School or on sports grounds, in trade unions and the Labor Party, in the achievement of Federation and the Liberal experiment of nation-building after 1901.

National values

Gordon Greenwood's Jubilee history, *Australia*, was a self-conscious 'Australian' departure from the English tradition of historical writing. This was represented, for example by Englishman Ernest Scott at the University of Melbourne, who not surprisingly located Australian history within the larger framework of British imperialism. For Scott, British traditions were everything and British history was Australian history. 'It has stood for very much in the development of Australia', he wrote, 'that her people have been proud of their race and sensitive to maintain its best traditions. British history is their history.' The population itself was 'thoroughly British' as were its values.[12]

First published in 1916, Scott's *Short History of Australia* was revised in the 1920s to take account of the impact of World War 1. As official historian of the volume on the home front, Scott was mindful of its divisive impact on Australia, but he praised the Anzacs' achievement as an example of British 'valour'. Lest Australians show too much national pride in this military expedition, he reminded readers that 'English as well as Australian troops took part in the Gallipoli campaign'.[13]

In 1930 the historian WK Hancock also emphasised the importance of British traditions, but he discerned, too, the emergence in the new environment and circumstances of settlement a distinctive national ethos and set of values: 'the sentiment of justice, the claim of right, the conception of equality'.[14] Contemporary fiction writers and playwrights such as Vance and Nettie Palmer, Louis Esson and Katharine Susannah Prichard (whose returned soldier husband Hugo Throssell committed suicide) also turned their backs on the war, when it came to defining national distinctiveness, writing stories and plays that emphasised the nation-building role of pioneering the outback and the new communities battling the bush. Ironically these outback pioneers have been retrospectively re-cast in a 2009 essay on 'The Spirit of Anzac' by retired Lieutenant Colonel Arthur Burke as the earliest exemplars of the Anzac spirit.[15]

Katharine Prichard – who like many of her friends was active in the anti-war movement – was deeply influenced by the war experience of her husband and brother, whose letters home told of the terrible waste of lives:

Describing a futile attack and the men dead and dying as a result of it, he wrote, 'someone has blundered!' and later: 'I begin to agree with many of your ideas ... War is a rotten business. A way must be found to stop it ever happening again.'[16]

In the middle decades of the twentieth century most Australians had direct experience of the horror and waste of war and were thus less likely to romanticise or sentimentalise it.

In these years historians looked to Australia's political and social history for inspiration. Greenwood's *Australia* was the main Australian history text used by teachers and lecturers from the 1950s well into the 1970s. The preface explained that the broad aim of the book, written for the 'layman' as well as the 'specialist' was to write 'a political and social history of Australian society which would show the many-sided nature of its development at any given time'.[17] Greenwood wrote about the formative nation-building period between 1901 and 1930, which included chapters on World War 1 and the 1920s. Although he wrote at length about the AIF's military engagements, noting the soldiers' reputation for 'initiative and aggression', Greenwood's account of national development was not animated by 'the spirit of Anzac', but by an 'Australian ethos' that found its voice in nationalist literature in the late nineteenth century and social experimentation in the early twentieth.

Frank Crowley's *New History of Australia* published in 1974 during the time of the Whitlam government followed Greenwood in failing to register the role of the Anzac spirit in animating national history. The book contains just one (casual) reference to Anzac Day: in his chapter on the post-World War 2 period, 1939–51, Geoffrey Bolton notes that the Charles

Chauvel film *Forty Thousand Horsemen* (1940) became 'staple fare' on Anzac Day afternoons.[18] In his chapter on World War 1, Ian Turner, who had himself served in the army in World War 2 described the heroism of the diggers at Gallipoli largely in terms of their anti-heroic behaviour: they were undisciplined, they 'whinged continually' about their conditions and they were racist, one of them asking why 'Should White Australia defend Black Egypt?'[19] CEW Bean was cast here not as a champion of the diggers, but as their censorious critic, whose 'unpopularity among the soldiers took a long time to live down'.[20] Besides Bean was an upper middle class Anglophile.

The achievement of the Anzacs in Turner's account was not to establish military values as national values, but rather to demonstrate 'the established values of the bush'. Here Turner followed Russel Ward who had argued in his classic *The Australian Legend* that the Australian ethos was born among the outback pastoral workers and later projected onto the soldiers by Bean and other commentators. The *New History of Australia* also noted the emergence of the RSL on the right wing of politics in the 1920s to become 'the most powerful pressure group in Australia for years to come'.[21] Spokesmen for returned soldiers were conservative and imperialist in their politics and attracted little sympathy from left-leaning historians. The prominence of the RSL in Australian political life for much of the twentieth century caused many writers and historians to distance themselves from the Anzac legend.

Melbourne historian Stuart Macintyre in his volume of the *Oxford History of Australia,* published in 1986, followed Ian Turner in characterising the Anzacs in unflattering terms. He noted their bravery and solidarity, but also that the 'digger was bombastic and self-aggrandizing, given to contempt for the British officer and intolerant of others with whom the war threw him into contact, yet not unresponsive to flattery'.[22] Macintyre also followed Turner in noting Bean's disapproval of the soldiers' loutish behaviour, quoting his observation that 'I think we have to admit that our force contains more bad hats than the others'.[23] The champion of the ideal Anzac, Bean was clearly more ambivalent about and uncomfortable with the behaviour of real diggers.

With an emphasis on political history, Macintyre argues that out of this 'nation divided' by war emerged a stronger sense of nationality, but that this was the work of Prime Minister WM Hughes at an international level, determined to give voice to and secure Australian interests, in particular the protection of the White Australia Policy at the Peace Conference at Versailles. Hughes posed as 'the little digger', the friend of the Anzacs, but returned soldiers exercised a reactionary influence in politics that alienated many potential members of the Returned Sailors' and Soldiers' Imperial League of Australia (RSSILA), which by 1924, represented only nine per cent of all ex-servicemen. Anzacs were a divided and divisive political force in post-war Australia and their official representatives in the RSSILA spoke for explicitly conservative values.

The radical nationalists whose work was influential in the 1960s and 1970s, Bob Gollan, Ian Turner, Geoff Serle and Russel Ward, wrote an Australian history that emphasised the role of those on the left of politics – labour men, bush-workers, trade unionists, republicans, nationalist poets and writers – in forging a sense of national identity and contributing to the idea of nationhood. To the extent that the Anzacs could be part of this story it was not because of their 'baptism of fire', but because they were bearers of the values of the bush, the egalitarian Australian ethos.

In the 1970s and 1980s, this celebratory national narrative began to be discredited by a powerful combination of younger historians, critical of its sexism and racism. 'Australians are now increasingly discovering their past', wrote Miriam Dixson in 1976. 'But the explorers are mainly males and what they are uncovering tends to concern the lives and achievements of males ... Thus in this proud democracy, women figure as pygmies in the culture of the present and are almost obliterated from the annals of the past.'[24] Other historians such as Humphrey McQueen, Ann Curthoys and CD Rowley were pointing to the racism that had in different ways underpinned the growth of the proud democracy. It was clearly the case that the Australian vision of equal opportunity and social justice, as it had been elaborated in the last years of the nineteenth century and the first decades of the twentieth century, had been integrally linked to the insistent demand for racial homogeneity. Democratic equality had meant racial exclusion. As WK Hancock wrote in 1930: 'The policy of White Australia is the indispensable condition of every other Australian policy.'[25]

It was the White Australia Policy that distinguished Australia from Britain in 1901 and underpinned assertions of sovereignty; it was the White Australia Policy, as Alfred Deakin had proclaimed, that was the founding creed of our nationality. Just as new histories of Aboriginal dispossession and Aboriginal activism made it increasingly difficult to persevere with Australia Day as a day of national celebration, as we show in chapter five, so de-colonisation and multiculturalism demanded the final repudiation of the national ideal of White Australia. Thus a vacuum opened up at the heart of the national story. There was a longing for a proud national history, which would be duly met by the revivification of the myth of Anzac.

New social histories such as Bill Gammage's fine study *The Broken Years* (1974) and Patsy Adam-Smith's popular *The Anzacs* (1978), drawing on soldiers' own diaries and letters, paved the way. In particular they would play a crucial role in establishing the innocent young soldier as the face of Anzac, the beautiful boys in the film *Gallipoli*, Archie and Frank, replacing the reactionary visage of Bruce Ruxton, the omnipresent and vociferous president of the Victorian branch of the RSL.

In these new histories, Anzacs were no longer the aggressive and skilled wielders of the bayonet, vividly rendered in Ellis Ashmead-Bartlett's eyewitness account in 1915, but the victims of war – and of the British. 'War is hell', wrote Patsy Adam-Smith, but 'we must remember not to castigate the victims of war – and every man who fights is a victim'.[26]

One of the most perceptive commentaries on the implications of the historical return to Anzac was provided by historian Manning Clark. His account of the birth of the Anzac legend in volume 5 of *History of Australia* was also a comment on his own times: 'Some Australians were abandoning their hopes of creating a society free of the evils of the old world, a society where there was equality of opportunity without servility, mediocrity, or greyness of spirit.' But the turn to Anzac Day as 'Australia's day of glory', he wrote, had made the nation 'a prisoner of her past, rather than an architect of a new future for humanity. The story of the heroism would be told for generations to come. So the founding ideals of Australia had been "cast to the winds".'[27]

Manning Clark proved prescient. With the proliferation of military histories, from the 1980s, national traditions that had incorporated ideals of a more just society were lost to sight. In 1980 an 'Australians at War cassette' offered 'the complete history of Australia's fighting forces – the courage – the humour – the pathos – the patriotism – through song and verse and yarn'.[28] This would be soon complemented by all kinds of military history: the personal accounts of nurses and infantrymen, studies of women at war and prisoners of war, books about the Boer War, World Wars 1 and 2, the Pacific war, Papua New Guinea, the Middle East, the Malayan Emergency, Korea, Vietnam, the Gulf and Afghanistan. Leading journalists such as Les Carlyon, Paul Ham and Peter FitzSimons made this fertile field their own.

In *What's Wrong with Anzac?* we analyse these movements in Australian history and changes in Australian self-definition. We address the questions of how and why the myth of Anzac has acquired a central place in Australian history and public memory. We show that the rewriting of Australian history has required forgetting as well as remembering. We look at how the desire to recognise those who fought for their country has led not just to proper reward and reparation, but also to the militarisation of Australian history, public memory and national values.

Central to this process has been the transformation of military history into family history, an enterprise made possible by the vast new genealogical resources, including Nominal Rolls, available at the Australian War Memorial and the Department of Veterans' Affairs. In no other country has military experience in foreign wars become so central to a nation's sense of itself and its national identity. The War of Independence in North America is commemorated because of its profound political significance in inaugurating a new political and social order. In the American war against the British empire, the United States founded an independent republic, the first post-colonial republic in the world. In 1915 our soldiers went to fight for the British empire and its allies, the French and Russians, in their war against the German and Austro-Hungarian empires. Rather than inaugurating a new phase of national independence between the wars, Gallipoli served to lock Australia more firmly into the Imperial embrace. Following World War 1, British values, education, literature and even the British accent were re-invigorated in Australia.

Critical analyses of the Anzac legend, as we have seen, risk inciting charges of disloyalty and treason. Thus we ask whether the cult of Anzac is now creating two classes of citizen in a process that ironically reflects the divisions opened up in World War 1. At that time, lines were drawn between 'enlisted men' and those stigmatised as 'shirkers'. This has now been re-cast as a division between those who themselves or whose relatives went to war – and thus have a right to speak – and those who haven't earned this right and must remain silent. As became evident on the *Age* blog people now feel obliged to preface any remarks about Anzac with a statement of their family's military service.

Finally, we raise the question of whether the militarisation of our national values – and the proliferation of commemorative days, war memorials and military history – has naturalised our condition of always being at war and thus silenced debate about our participation in current and future wars. When did we last read or hear public debates about whether we should be in the ever more destructive war in Afghanistan? Is our military commitment there simply an extension of our 'civilising' role in Iraq and the Middle East? Writing in the *Age* blog, Dean was troubled by the lack of discussion and clarity: '[George] Orwell's state sponsored never ending war is so close to a reality, does any of us even know who we are fighting, where and why? We just know we're always at war ...'

–1–

Are nations really made in war?

Henry Reynolds

'War is the living fountain from which flows
the entire society.'

WG Sumner, *War and Other Essays*, Yale University Press,
New Haven, 1911, p 16

They were quite certain, even emphatic, in their views. And it
seemed there was little dissent, although not everyone spoke. I
had been asked to talk to a group of bright, enthusiastic senior
high school students about Anzac Day and had begun by asking
them to tell me why they thought it was important. Two ideas
dominated their response. The Anzac landing had made Australia a nation and the young diggers had shown a spirit that
was inimitably Australian. These answers didn't surprise me.
It was, indeed, hard to imagine how a class like this one anywhere in contemporary Australia would have come up with
other answers, so pervasive was the common view and so constantly repeated in speeches, articles, lectures and lessons.

Leaders in all walks of life affirmed this interpretation of the
Anzac landing, even if they disagreed about many other things

and they had been doing so across the years. The interpretation had been sanctified by reiteration. As leading war historian Peter Stanley observed recently, the Gallipoli campaign

> occupies a central place in Australia's national mythology, identity and memory. The landing on the Peninsula has been portrayed by commentators across the political spectrum as representing the place and time when Australia became a nation.[1]

This view is now so powerful and so pervasive that it is rarely questioned. To do so is to show inexcusable disrespect for the dead. Dissent in such a case has rarely been tolerated and as we have noted has provoked accusations of treason. But the idea that the Anzac landing made the nation has raised so many questions and is such a problematic claim it's a wonder that it has remained for so long beyond the reach of criticism. I suggested to the class that the proposition they favoured could only be tested by considering what had happened both before and after the landing and by an assessment of how and when nations are made and the role of war in that process.

Rhetoric and reality

Historical reality confounds the rhetoric. If the Anzacs made the nation what does this say about the first hundred years of settlement? Was it all merely preparatory, just a prelude? Was there nothing that happened within the Australian colonies before 1915 that had the importance of the Anzac landing? Could the Commonwealth of Australia fairly be described as an inadequate nation? By any measure it was a remarkably successful society, the envy of many countries in the contemporary world. It was peaceful, well governed and prosperous. The average family was better nourished, housed and educated than in almost any other society. For more than half a century the self-governing colonies had developed their economies and their institutions and had introduced progressive reforms which had placed them at the forefront of democratic advance.

The tradition was carried through into the first years of the new Commonwealth, which introduced women's rights, a living wage, old age pensions and kindred measures which pioneered the welfare state. This story of progressive, innovative legislation was recognised by well-informed contemporaries in Britain, continental Europe and North America. And at the time the White Australia Policy that underpinned these advances was widely admired and emulated. Federated Australia was a collective achievement; the slow cumulative work of innumerable citizens in all walks of life. If all this had failed to create a nation what new, missing element, was added by the young men who invaded Turkey in 1915? The only possible answer is that fighting is more important to the life of nations than farming or legislating, labouring, teaching, nurturing children or any other of the innumerable, unspectacular activities of civil society.

And what of the country after April 1915? War did not unite, but rather divided society. Australia was far more deeply divided in 1919 than it had been in 1914. War tore at the social fabric. The two campaigns fought over the issue of conscription in 1916 and 1917 were bitter affairs, prising apart communities, congregations and families, ruining previously enduring friendships. Class conflict was accentuated and strikes broke out across the country. The fault line between Catholic and Protestant was widened by the Easter Rising in Dublin in 1916 and further exacerbated by the conscription referenda. And as soldiers returned they came into conflict with those who had stayed at home.

Within a few years of the end of the war, Western Australia made a serious attempt to leave the federation, the shared experience of war notwithstanding. And it would be hard to argue that Australia became more independent in the 1920s and 1930s. If anything loyalty to Crown and empire became more rather than less pronounced. If the war had made Australians more self-confident there was little to show for it in the decades between the wars. The bond with king and empire had been sealed and sanctified in blood. The drive by the dominions to achieve independence from Britain was initiated by Canada, South Africa and Ireland. Loyal Australia followed reluctantly in their wake.

Any discussion of the evolution of Australian nationalism comes up against the inescapable problem of sovereignty. Australia was not an independent nation state either before or after 1915. It had no control of its foreign policy, no diplomatic service and the monarch remained the Head of State. The national government had no say in the decision as to where the Australian Imperial Force (AIF) would go, who it would fight and for what reasons of state they would kill and be killed. Australia couldn't even choose its own enemies. The political and strategic decisions were made in London and the detail of Imperial policy was not necessarily divulged to Australian leaders. This had the paradoxical result of totally obscuring the question of Australia's own national interest.

If Australia only had the most general reasons for going to war how could success or failure be measured? In some ways this gave an aura of purity to the great sacrifice. It was unsullied by political calculation. Success would be calibrated not by measurable political or strategic achievement, but by the display of character, of courage and stoicism and by the metaphorical creation of a nation. Anything less would make the sacrifice seem more unbearable. The thought that so many young men had died in vain could not be countenanced by grieving families, returned men or the leaders who decided to send them overseas. Such a large sacrifice must have been worthwhile. Anyone who suggested otherwise would attract intense opprobrium.

Killing and dying

The belief that nations are made in war provokes many troubling thoughts. I only alluded to a few when talking to the high school students. They are necessarily and inescapably confronting. But the silence on the subject, so marked in Australia, will not make them go away. Is war, for instance, the only, or even the most direct avenue to national maturity? Does a seasoning war need to be a just one or will any war do? Do nations who have lived in peace lack something important? And how does violence contribute to a nation's spirit or identity? Australia's Anzac rhetoric dwells on suffering endured, but what of suffering inflicted? Sacrifice and dying are admired, but what about the killing? It seems we rarely talk about it. I'm sure the class members found the subject troubling and distasteful. But it cannot be avoided if we talk about war. As Joanna Bourke's first sentence of her recent book *An Intimate History of Killing* states:

> The characteristic act of men at war is not dying, it is
> killing. For politicians, military strategists and many
> historians, war may be about the conquest of territory or the

struggle to recover a sense of national honour but for the man on active service warfare is concerned with the lawful killing of other people.[2]

Was Australia's much celebrated coming of age in 1915 consummated by the killing of Turks? Were the Anzacs applauded because they were good at it? All the courage and bravery in the world meant little if they were not employed in the brutal business of killing. They can't stand alone without a consideration of their purpose or the circumstances which call them into life. Is that what lies latent inside the common discourse of the period about the Australians being blooded at Gallipoli? And what are we to make of all the talk about manhood which has been so common in Australian rhetoric about war? Did the real man need blood on his hands? The historical record shows quite clearly that soldiers who shrank from the bloody business were commonly thought to be cowards, to be less than men.

The inseparable fusion of heroism and killing can be found in the famous early accounts of the landing at Anzac Cove. The first, and by far the most influential, was by the English war correspondent Ellis Ashmead-Bartlett, which appeared in Australia on 8 May 1915. More than any other report it launched the legend of Anzac. There had been, he told his avid readers, 'no finer feat in this war' than the landing at Gallipoli, while the courage of the wounded was such that it would, 'never be forgotten'. But his enthusiasm stemmed from the Australians' élan most characteristically displayed in their enthusiasm for bayoneting Turks. When their blood was up, he observed, 'this race of athletes … rushed northwards and eastwards, searching for fresh enemies to bayonet'.[3]

The questions I posed to the students about war and its celebration are difficult to deal with, but they graphically illustrate the problems which arise when we continue to employ today the language and ideas of another era. The cherished rhetoric of 1915 carries with it the militaristic ideas of the Edwardian world as it had been before the outbreak of World War 1. And while at contemporary Anzac Day celebrations, speakers ritually condemn war, the old rhetoric gestures in the opposite direction. It continues to refer to nobility, sacrifice and the role of the soldier in the creation of the nation.

The duty of manhood

In discussion with the students, we agreed that in the past many authoritative figures had declared that the nation was born on the shores of the Gallipoli Peninsula (also now known as the Anzac Peninsula). This view was widely held. Clergymen, politicians, poets, mayors and business leaders all clustered in common chorus. Anzac Day, announced the Anglican archbishop of Sydney in 1916, 'gave Australia her soul'.[4] The *Sydney Morning Herald* declared that the nation had cast on one side the ideas and ideals of adolescence and 'assumed the serious responsibilities of Man's estate'.[5] The Hobart *Mercury* was similarly convinced that at Gallipoli, Australia 'had taken up the duties of manhood'. Australians had become a 'blood brotherhood in the best sense'.[6] The Sydney Roman Catholic paper, *Freeman's Journal* declared that: 'we are at last a nation, with one heart, one soul and one thrilling aspiration'.[7]

A common theme ran through much of the rhetoric. War was the ultimate test both of men and nations. The battlefield was the site where they succeeded or failed. Like steel they were tempered or consumed in the fire of conflict. The poet

AB Patterson had written:

> The mettle that a race can show
> Is proved with shot and steel,
> And now we know what nations know
> And feel what nations feel.[8]

And much of the language of 1915 was carried through into the post-war period. The author of a 1921 book about Anzac celebrations in Queensland wrote that 25 April was the day on which Australia became entitled, 'through an ordeal of blood, fire, and suffering to take her place among the great nations of the world'.[9] In his official history of the war published between 1921 and 1942, CEW Bean declared that on the battlefields Australia faced 'the one trial that ... all humanity still recognizes – the test of a great war'.[10]

Another theme which ran through much of the rhetoric about war was that conflict had a purifying effect on society, turning the citizen's attention away from pleasure, leisure and material advancement to the more serious, the more spiritual aspects of life. It made society more earnest, banished frivolity and purged Australian life of 'its intemperance, uncleanness, mutual distrust, commercial dishonesty, political chicanery'.[11] Such hopes were voiced in serial sermons during the early years of the war and were taken up by Prime Minister WM Hughes who argued:

> Since it has evoked this pure and noble spirit who shall
> say that this dreadful war is wholly an evil? Into a world
> saturated with a lust of material things, which had elevated
> self into a diety, which had made wealth the standard of
> greatness, comes the sweet purifying breath of self sacrifice.[12]

Clearly then, many Australians believed in 1915 that nations were made in war, that armed conflict was the supreme test for both men and their societies. Several important questions therefore present themselves. Why were these views so common at the time, were they contested by contemporaries and should we today (almost a hundred years later) still echo the accompanying and dated rhetoric?

Edwardian militarism

Perhaps the most difficult thing to explain to a contemporary audience is the extent to which the symbolism, ceremony and language of Anzac relate back to the ideas current in Europe and North America in the years before 1914 and the intense and incessant debates about war which characterised the era. At the turn of the century both Britain and the United States were involved in wars. The United States fought Spain, driving her out of Cuba and the Philippines while Britain conquered the two Boer Republics in South Africa with the assistance of troops from Australia. Both wars were controversial, evoking both ecstatic support and intense criticism, and serious consideration about the place of war in the life of modern nations. At the same time there was both an increasingly expensive arms race and the introduction of universal conscription in almost every country in Europe with the exception of Britain itself. War was constantly discussed in the books and journals of the period. Militarists urged governments to spend ever more money on armies and navies, warned of impending dangers and talked of both the terrible, inescapable necessity and the ageless nobility of war.

Running like a warming current through much heated rhetoric were ideas drawn from the innumerable popular accounts of Social Darwinists. Applied, and just as often misapplied to society, they suggested that nations like the species of the natural world were governed by the iron laws of evolution and were inescapably driven into ceaseless struggle and competition. The fit would survive and triumph; the weak would be crushed and swept aside. War was the principal means of struggle and therefore an ugly necessity which nonetheless brought forth the most selfless devotion to the nation. Such ideas were heard and held in much of Europe, the United States and the British dominions. The leading international jurist of the age, TJ Lawrence, alluded to the contemporary doctrine which held 'that nations cannot long retain their manly virtues of courage and endurance unless their populations are from time to time disciplined in the hard school of war ...'[13] In Britain the history professor JA Cramb wrote in 1914 that in war man had a possession which he 'values above religion, above industry and above social comfort' because it provided the power which 'it affords to life of rising above life'.[14]

The book in question, *Germany and England* was an immense success and was reprinted ten times in three months. In a follow up text, *The Origin and Destiny of Imperial Britain*, published posthumously in 1915, Cramb was even more lyrical. The shaping, all pervading thought of the book was of 'the might, majesty, and the mystery of war'. Armed conflict brought with it the 'intensification of life'. The battlefield, he declared, was, 'an altar; the sacrifice the most awful the human eye can contemplate or the imagination with all its efforts invent'.[15] The leading British military figure Colonel FN Maude held similar views. War was necessary to society because it was like a cleansing fever. It cleared away the 'foulness of the body national and patriotic, and its renewed life is thereafter stronger in proportion as the ordeal has been drastic'.[16] For one of Maude's military colleagues, CH Melville, war was the 'supreme test of virility'; for another it was 'God's test of a nation's soul'.[17]

Senior serving British officers held similar views. General Sir Ian Hamilton, who was to command the Gallipoli campaign, declared in 1906 that it was the 'heroism, self sacrifice and chivalry' which redeemed war and would 'build up national character'.[18] But by far the most powerful voice was that of Lord Frederick Roberts, military hero and commander in chief until 1905 when he stepped down to become president of the influential National Service League. Without war, the great man declared,

> a nation is in risk of running to seed. And when the war is a just one ... its benefit to the nation is great. It is an appeal to the manhood and the virtue of the people. It prevents decadence and effeminacy. It corrects the selfishness and querulousness which are inevitably bred by a long peace.
>
> We are all tried by fire are we not? A nation needs to be tried by fire – needs to be put on trial every now and then, and tested by the laws which govern this planet – the law I mean, particularly, that only the efficient survive.[19]

The views of men like Roberts and Hamilton were widely known in Australia and often referred to in local debates. They carried an aura of aristocratic authority and of hard won experience on the empire's diverse battlefields.

Australian leaders who read the books of the period and the articles in the leading contemporary reviews from Europe or the United States were constantly reminded of the intense debate about war and its role in the life of society. The works of conti nental European soldiers and scholars were frequently translated and published in Britain. German writing about war, though much condemned at the time in the English speaking world, had little to say that stands out from the militarist declarations commonly heard in Britain, the United States and Australia. The historian and notorious Prussian militarist, Heinrich von Treitschke had many things to say about war that sit comfortably with the rhetoric of Anzac. 'Only in war' he wrote, 'does a nation become a nation'. He talked much of the sacrifice 'of fellow countrymen for one another' which was nowhere, 'so splendidly exhibited as in war'.

And those who died well should be treated as heroes. 'It is the heroes of the nation', he declared, 'who are the figures that delight and inspire youthful minds'; and among authors it is those whose words that ring 'like the sound of trumpets whom as boys and youths we most admire'. Anyone who did not rejoice in stories of the nation's military heroes was 'too cowardly to bear arms'. Treitschke also wrote about killing and the masculine camaraderie Australians called mateship:

> We have learned to know the moral majesty of war in the very thing that appears brutal and inhumane to superficial observers. That one must overcome the natural feelings of humanity for the sake of the fatherland, that in this case men murder one another who have never harmed one another before and who perhaps esteem one another highly as chivalrous enemies, that is at first glance the awfulness of war, but at the same time its greatness also ...
>
> If we pursue this idea further we recognize that war, with all its sternness and roughness, also weaves a bond of love between men, since here all class distinctions vanish, and the risk of death knits man to man.[20]

A great deal of evidence supports the Prussian thinker's claims about the bonds between men. In all armies the story was the same.[21] The heroic rhetoric of 1914 did not survive the horrors of modern warfare, but the bonding of comrades remained to provide the emotional sustenance which allowed men to endure.

In his celebrated history of World War 1 John Keegan observed that men whom the trenches 'cast into intimacy entered into bonds of mutual dependency and sacrifice of self stronger than any of the friendships made in peace and better times'.[22] There is no doubt about the importance of mateship in the AIF. But the mistake is to present mateship as something inimitably, even uniquely Australian. Even the word 'mate' was commonly in use in contemporary Britain. As early as 1914 the liberal scholar Gilbert Murray was celebrating the fact that the mateship common among 'working men' was becoming more general. 'The ice between man and man is broken now' he announced, 'we are now a band of brothers standing side by side'.[23] The German cavalry officer Rudolph Binding similarly wrote of the sense of comradeship he experienced at the outbreak of war because men:

> were equal. No-one wished to count for more than anyone else. On the streets and avenues men looked each other in the eye and rejoiced in their togetherness.[24]

The pacifist rejoinder

War, then, was on the mind of the Western world in the years before 1914. But many people devoted their energies to opposing militarism and supporting the powerful international peace movement. The jurist TJ Lawrence observed:

> Among the most extraordinary phenomena of modern times we may reckon the simultaneous growth of the material preparations for warfare and a sentiment of horror and reprobation of war. Both are apparent all over the civilized world.[25]

Peace activists looked with hope to the International Peace Congresses held at the Hague in 1899 and 1907. Much debate took place about the future role of international law and the use of mediation to settle disputes between nations. Captains of industry like Andrew Carnegie and Alfred Nobel invested in peace. The Nobel Peace Prize was inaugurated in 1901. The peace movement in Britain was energised by opposition to the Boer War which drew in many of the most prominent liberal intellectuals and politicians. The National Peace Council brought together assorted political, religious and industrial organisations which met at national congresses at Bristol in 1905 and Cardiff in 1909. Activity peaked at the time of the Universal Peace Congress in London in the summer of 1908.[26] The Australian peace movement had links with comparable bodies in Britain, but it was unable to exert an equal measure of influence on public life.

Pacifists drew inspiration from many, and often contradictory, sources. They attacked contemporary militarism on many fronts. Perhaps the most enduring was the objective assessment of the likely cost of prolonged war fought with modern weapons. The most prophetic and most chilling was the work of the Polish industrialist IS Bloch whose book *Is War Now Possible* was published in England in 1899. A powerful corrective to romanticism about war, Bloch argued with technical expertise and dark foreboding that modern war would be prolonged and immensely destructive. He correctly foresaw that the firepower of modern armies would lead to the stalemate of the Western Front and the enormous loss of life among any formations caught in no-man's land. It was a message that many ignored. The English journalist Norman Angell provided the peace movement with a powerful and immensely popular book called *The Great Illusion* first published in 1909 and subsequently reprinted many times. Angell argued that war made no sense among the great powers whose economies were closely integrated and mutually dependent and, like Bloch, he pointed out in detail the enormous damage which would result from a major war in Europe.

Running parallel with the warnings about the likely consequences of war, were attacks on the premises which underpinned much of the militarist literature. Popular Social Darwinism was turned on its head. War, it was argued, did not ensure the survival of the fittest but their destruction, leaving the feeble and the unfit to propagate the next generation. The American pacifist and scholar David Starr Jordan observed in 1915 that:

> The certainty that war leads towards racial decadence by the obliteration of the most virile elements these being thereby left unrepresented in heredity, is becoming widely accepted as the crucial argument against the war system of the world ...[27]

And the natural world did not provide evidence of conflict and killing within species but on the contrary those animals which co-operated were more likely to survive. Angell argued that the natural course for man was to establish the means for future co-operation and that the true struggle was with the natural environment not with each other.

The veneration of military heroism was also challenged along with the related claim that nations benefitted by war. The radical English scholar JA Hobson decried the 'false philosophy of history' which claimed support from 'misapplied biology' and had,

> imposed on a large semi-educated public the belief that
> a military and commercial struggle for existence and for
> predominance is a wholesome necessity in national life.[28]

Hobson called for Britain to direct a larger share of her 'thought, feeling and activity' to those works of internal development which were the 'wholesome food of patriotism'.[29] Fellow scholar GP Gooch decried the exaltation of military achievement and the 'relative disparagement of the more humdrum pursuits of civil life'. These were common sentiments at the time. Gooch also called into question the 'glorification of physical courage revealed in war' arguing that military courage was, in itself 'no surety for moral excellence' and it often existed in company 'with utter moral degradation'.[30]

The American pacifist General Hiram Chittenden, responding to writers who lauded military heroism, attacked what he called the 'warped conception' of true courage and heroism. He thought there was no more virtue in dying on the battlefield than in any other circumstance. 'What makes a man go into Battle?' he asked rhetorically. He thought it was seldom personal courage or patriotic fervour, observing that soldiers,

> must obey orders under severe penalties; their pride helps
> them for they hate to be called cowards and when the strife

is on fear vanishes in the excitement and wild passion of the moment. Men dying thus have no special claim to virtue. Each passing day calls forth, in the line of common duty acts of true heroism ... which entitle the actors to recognition as high and lasting as that accorded to the noblest deeds of war. It is a perversion of justice to hold in light esteem, as the world commonly does, the humble heroes of daily life and laud to the skies the heroes of camp and battlefield.[31]

A central concept that came under pacifist attack was the proposal that war made nations and made them great. 'Historically', LC Jane argued, 'it is idle to suggest that the mere fact of fighting ... has any beneficial effect upon national character'. Rather war called into vigorous life, 'the more degraded instincts of mankind'.[32] Angell directly addressed his many contemporaries who sang the praises of war as 'a valuable school of morals'. Did they believe ultimately that war of itself was desirable? Would they, he demanded to know, 'urge going to war unnecessarily or unjustly merely because it is good for us?'[33] But there were even more uncompromising voices than Angell's. DS Jordan declared in 1915 that murder remained murder even when done 'on a gigantic scale under the sanction of the state and the blessing of the church'.[34] He was writing before his country entered the war. Englishman George Bernard Shaw penned a similar passage at the height of the conflict on the Western Front:

When all is said that possibly can be said for the war, it is a monstrous crime against civilization and humanity; and the notion that any of the parties voluntarily engaged in it can be blameless is absurd. It is impossible to discuss war practically without a suspension of all ordinary morals and all normal religious and humanitarian pretensions. Even that is not enough: it is necessary to set up alongside of martial law ... an outrageous special morality and religion, in which murder becomes duty and patriotism ...[35]

But the views of pacifists like Shaw provoked mounting hostility as the bloody stalemate continued on the Western Front. Dissent was increasingly viewed as disloyalty; opposition to the war as treason. The introduction of conscription in Britain early in 1916 increased official pressure on conscientious objectors. Prominent opponents of the war like philosopher Bertrand Russell and journalist Fenner Brockway were imprisoned. Peace notes from the Vatican and Germany and plans for a socialist-led peace conference at Stockholm in 1917 all failed to stir the decision-makers. Pacifists were characterised by Australian Prime Minister WM Hughes as 'peace cranks ... and secret agents of Germany, masquerading as pacifists ... gathered together as a cunning trap'.[36] Pre-war pacifists turned their attention to plans for a new international organisation to be created when the guns eventually fell silent.

The after-life of Edwardian militarism

The twin ideas that both nations and their heroes are made in war were sharply contested before World War 1. The pacifists pointed out that they could not co-exist with a genuine condemnation of war or the desire to avoid it. If war tested men and nations, as many militarists declared, there must be some good in it. The heroism heralded on the battlefield, and worthy of both emulation and admiration, must be seen as the fine, exalted fruits of conflict. But after the experience of the

Western Front and the death and destruction of the war and its aftermath, the militarist writers of the Edwardian era were discredited and quickly forgotten. Glorification of war, fashionable before 1914, was eschewed in most combatant countries. It was left to Benito Mussolini, Adolf Hitler and the Japanese military to keep the worship of war alive during the 1930s. Defeat in World War 2 and the humiliation of occupation saw the final eclipse of attitudes to war widespread before 1914.

In Australia however tragedy was turned into glory through CEW Bean's promulgation of the Anzac legend. In his study of war writing called *Big-Noting*, Robin Gerster observed that war correspondents told Australians at home that the conflict was 'an exhilarating, if dangerous, adventure'.[37] Bean himself showed 'an old fashioned preference to look at the positive, the "bright," the heroic side of war'.[38] His prose was studded with sporting metaphors. Much Australian writing about the war in magazines such as *Lone Hand* (and indeed the mainstream media) suggested that Australians excelled, even revelled in battle and that the war hero was the apotheosis of Australian manhood. When the great wave of anti-war publications emerged between the wars – discussed in chapter three – the executive of the Returned Sailors' and Soldiers' Imperial League of Australia (RSSILA) raised the need to set up a system of censorship to be directed against the authors of war books 'who defame Australian soldiers'.[39]

The echoes of Edwardian militarism lived on however, in what Geoff Serle called 'the liturgy of Anzac Day'. The national investment in Anzac meant a continuing embrace of atavistic ideas about the importance of war in the life of nations. Without such ideas the Anzac landing would have lost its central significance in national mythology. Whether they should be passed on to our children with such determination should be a matter for serious consideration.

At the heart of the matter is Australia's distinctive military history which has all taken place overseas. Australia has been engaged in many wars in the last hundred years, but the fighting has occurred in other people's countries (with the exception of the attacks on Darwin). Our military forces have been involved in conflicts in Europe, North and South Africa, the Mediterranean, the Middle East, East and South-East Asia, recently in Iraq and currently in Afghanistan. But we have been spared the military occupation to which we have subjected others. Experience of war has, with the exception of Darwin, been confined to the military forces. The Pacific war against Japan barely touched mainland Australia. The continent has never been occupied and we have suffered very few civilian casualties.

In the past century we have not known war in the way that so many others have. We were spared the full horrors of the tumultuous twentieth century. In this way our experience is similar to that of the United States. In a recent article, 'What have we learned, if anything', the American historian, Tony Judt, sought to explain his country's currently bellicose attitude to war. The United States, he argued, was the only advanced democracy 'where public figures glorify and exult the military'. Such sentiments, familiar in Europe before 1945, were, he believed, quite unknown elsewhere today. The difference was that Europe and many countries in Asia and Africa had experienced invasion and devastation and had suffered enormous civilian casualties. Even Britain, although spared invasion, lost sixty-seven thousand civilian dead during World War 2. Those societies which had felt the full force of the horror of war understood war 'only too well'. Americans however had been 'fortunate enough to live in blissful ignorance of its true significance'.[40] Judt's observations about the United States are even more relevant to Australia because the United States did experience the trauma of a bitter and destructive civil war that cost six hundred and twenty thousand lives and its participation in World War 1 was followed by a protracted period of isolationism. Australia's distance from the battlefields helps us understand the reason for our continuing romanticism about war and repeated willingness to go to war in the present.

−2−

Colonial Cassandras:
Why weren't the warnings heeded?

Henry Reynolds

'Cassandra, fair as golden Venus standing on
Pergamus, caught sight of her dear father in his
chariot, and his servant that was the city's herald
with him. Then she saw him that was lying upon the
bier, drawn by the mules, and with a loud cry she
went about the city saying, "Come hither Trojans,
men and women, and look on Hector; if ever you
rejoiced to see him coming from battle when he was
alive, look now on him that was the glory of our city
and all our people."'

Homer, *The Iliad*, Book XXIV

Cassandra is one of the best-known characters to have come
down to us from Greek mythology. She was favoured by the
gods who bestowed on her the power to foresee the future. But
when she was defiant the gods decreed that while she retained
her power she would never be able to convince people that her
warnings were of any value, even though she accurately foretold
the fall and destruction of Troy. The colonial Cassandras were
the politicians who warned their contemporaries of the dangers

of becoming involved in Britain's wars in the late nineteenth and early twentieth centuries. They foresaw that it would inevitably lead to disaster. But few people took their warnings seriously and their dark foreboding was as little able to change the course of events as Cassandra's dire prophesies.

A peaceful prospect

It was not what Australians expected at the start of 1899. They looked forward to the coming of Federation with the hope of improved economic conditions, new political arrangements and the founding of national institutions. War was far from their minds. Sporadic conflict with the Aborigines continued on the ragged fringe of settlement. Metropolitan newspapers carried occasional short reports if Europeans had been killed and in 1900 the rampage of Aboriginal bushrangers Jimmy and Joe Governor in rural New South Wales attracted intense, prolonged interest. Australians had individually crossed the Tasman to fight the Maoris and in 1885 the New South Wales government had sent a small detachment to the Sudan to support the British expedition tasked with avenging the death of General Charles George Gordon. The expedition sailed from Circular Quay after marching through milling, enthusiastic crowds. But it arrived too late to see any action and returned with little fanfare and less glory. Seen from the perspective of the late 1890s it seemed an aberration and one not likely to be repeated.

Going to war

But by the end of 1899 Australia was, collectively, at war. All six colonies had committed troops to the conflict in South

Africa. The papers were full of reports of skirmishes and sieges and maps of the Cape of Good Hope, the Orange Free State and the Transvaal. Readers were coached in the evils of the Boers, the intransigence of the president Paul Kruger and the suffering of the so-called Uitlanders (the expatriate British migrant workers). There was surprisingly little reporting of the intense debate arising in Britain about the morality and the wisdom of the war involving many of the leading literary and intellectual figures of the age. The new federal government inherited the engagement and made its own commitment of troops at the end of 1901. It was a portentous decision. The involvement in wars overseas, the dispatch of the expeditionary force and the accompanying apotheosis of the warrior all became deeply characteristic of twentieth century Australia. Indeed among the world's small powers Australia must have earned pre-eminence for being involved in more wars in more parts of the world than any other comparable country. It was not something that could have been foreseen in 1899. Neither history nor geography suggested such a militant destiny. A century which had seen war scares but no war and a geographical position remote from the world's trouble spots beckoned in the opposite direction. Why twentieth century Australia took such a decisive, militant turn still remains a question of great significance. It has been often described, but never fully explained.

A minority of colonial politicians did see the dangers of the involvement in the Sudan in 1885 and in South Africa in 1899–1902 and pleaded with their colleagues to avoid a path which they predicted would lead inescapably to engagement in future, unforseen conflict. Such views were seen by their contemporaries as, at best, displays of irritating dissent or, at worst, as disloyalty. They were in a minority in all seven parliaments which debated the commitment of troops and their importance has, consequently, been overlooked. But their arguments are worth re-considering and in many ways have more contemporary resonance than the opinions of their more conventional colleagues. For convenience it will be best to begin with the debate in New South Wales in 1885 before considering the much more extensive discussions of 1899–1901.

The responsibilities of empire

Supporters of the commitment advanced arguments which were to be heard again in 1899 and 1914 and which in modified form are still used to justify overseas engagements. Membership of the empire carried responsibilities as well as rights. An attack on Britain was an attack on New South Wales; humiliation of the Mother Country was humiliation of the colonies. The enemies of the Queen were the enemies of Englishmen everywhere. Australia's security was totally dependent on the maintenance of Britain's power and prestige. The colonists were at one with Britain heart and hand. Perhaps even more to the point was the powerful belief that Australia and Britain were united by race and the ties of blood which were more important than political borders or constitutional arrangements. But the Australian colonies had much to gain from involvement in war. The advantages were outlined in 1885. With the expedition to the Sudan, New South Wales had come of age and its real history had just begun. WH Holborow declared in the parliament: 'Now this country has risen to the stature of nationhood. And we are a nation's parliament henceforth.' The sense of excitement was hard to escape. The veteran politician, Sir John Robertson confessed that never in his long life did his blood 'so thrill with emotion' as when he saw the crowds farewell the soldiers. There were many contemporary declarations of loyalty and references to the bonds of kinship. But there was calculation as well, Robertson remarking that whatever the rights or wrongs of the matter he held that, 'if we expect England to stand by us in any trouble we ought to stand by England in her troubles'.[1] EA Baker made the same point:

> Depend upon it if the time comes – and God knows how near it may be – when the Australian colonies shall be in danger from a foreign foe. Englishmen will never forget the handsome way in which New South Wales offered this small assistance to them in their time of danger. Well I think great benefit will arise to the colony in that way.[2]

How will it end?

But it was indeed the precedent which worried the small band of dissenters. 'Can anyone say', asked James Fletcher, 'where this sending our men to fight in a foreign land will end, or what the expense may be?'[3] His colleague AJ Gould wondered how long the war might last and how great the commitment could become. But there was a larger question to face:

> We have, therefore, to look at the future liability, at the great departure we have taken, and also to remember that we have laid down the principle that we are now prepared to enter into England's wars, and to assist her with troops. Having done it now we shall be expected to do it again in the future.[4]

'Will it end in this one act?', asked the radical David Buchanan, 'or shall we not be bound to interfere in all of England's quarrels?' And the problem was that if the Imperial connection was maintained, 'every enemy of England became an enemy of ours'. The ties with Britain were a liability and a source of danger. He assumed that Britain would inevitably come into conflict with one of the great European powers and in those circumstances the colony would be committed in advance:

We can see at a glance how absurd the whole action is. But what was the use of sending assistance to England unless we are prepared to continue it … If you bind yourself to replace them, [soldiers killed or wounded] what an enormous burden will you fasten on the people of the country, and into what a fearful abyss of misery and wretchedness you will plunge the whole country.

The duty of the colonists was to 'stand upon this ground' and never send a soldier from their shores. Their obligation was to defend themselves against attack by repelling invaders. There was no duty to do anything else.[5] Several dissenting members took the view that New South Wales hitherto had an implicit policy of neutrality and had ports that were open to every country in the world. 'We have been neutral', declared Fletcher, 'neutrality has been our safeguard'. The colony had been at peace with the whole world. But with the commitment to the Sudan all that had changed:

What have we done now? We have published to the world that New South Wales is prepared to assist in fighting the battles of England whether England is in the right or in the wrong. We have thrown down the gauntlet, and who will dare say that other nations will not retaliate when the proper time arrives.[6]

The dissenting minority expressed a deep concern about where the military venture would ultimately lead. MJ Hammond predicted that it would 'involve the country ever after in European complications that we should be much better free from'. What good, he asked, could the colony gain by becoming wantonly mixed up with the 'hereditary troubles of England?' By venturing far from Australia's shores the government had compromised the country's isolation which was its greatest asset. Angus Cameron regretted that by 'foolishly thrusting ourselves to the front' the government had compromised our geographical position which 'almost gave us immunity from an attack from an enemy'.[7]

But it was James Buchanan who asked the questions which probed the morality of the intervention itself and questioned the right of the Australian colonists to involve themselves in countries half a world away. He is worth quoting at length:

> I said that the war was an unjust war. The Arabs are fighting
> for their liberties … What patriotism, then, is it in our
> soldiers to go and fight against those patriots, who have
> never done them any harm, and have no … desire to do
> them harm. If we were fighting for our rights and liberties
> against an infamous government and a foreign state which
> had no part in the matter came to fight against us, how
> would we relish it? … Our troops are called patriots by
> fighting against men who have never done harm to them and
> have never seen them in the face.[8]

Buchanan gestured to one of the persistent criticisms of those who have opposed many of Australia's military ventures overseas. There was, at the time, demonstrably no immediate or direct threat to Australia. The putative enemies had no capacity to harm Australia and no interest in doing so. The soldiers sent overseas knew nothing about the country where they were sent to fight or about the culture of their would-be opponents. Their antipodean innocence made them more than normally receptive to whatever propaganda the Imperial authorities wished at the time to propagate. The colonial politicians had neither the means nor the capacity or, often enough, even the interest, to assess the judgment of the Imperial government or the legitimacy of the conflict in question.

War on the Veldt

The fear of the few in 1885 that a precedent was being established was borne out in 1899. While preparing the ground for war against the Boer Republics the secretary of state for the colonies, Joseph Chamberlain, sought the armed assistance of the white settler colonies. He needed their political support to counter opposition to the venture within Britain itself. Using the colonial governors and the senior British military officers, serving in Australia, he solicited, and eventually received, what was made out to be a spontaneous expression of colonial loyalty.[9] The problem for the colonial governments was that if one held back this would give the impression of disloyalty. All of the colonies fell into line, even little Tasmania. A message of thanks from the old Queen sprang the diplomatic trap. Realpolitik was wreathed in royalist sentimentality.

The commitments were supported in all the colonial parliaments with varying degrees of dissent and popular, but by no means universal enthusiasm was expressed in the first two years of the war. As in New South Wales, in 1885, the proponents of war had a ready collection of arguments. Above all else was the affirmation of loyalty to either the Queen, or Britain or to both. It was a gesture which silenced critics and circumvented the need for further thought. The morality of the war, the rights and the wrongs of the case, being vigorously thrashed out in Britain itself, could be ignored. The less one knew about the diplomatic politics the better. A telling exchange took place in the Western Australian parliament in 1899 when the commitment was being discussed. Frederick Illingworth regretted that any discussion on the question should take place at all. JRA Connolly said that the questions about South African politics should have no effect on the local parliament, it being a matter 'we may safely leave to the Imperial authorities at Home'. It was an observation which elicited a loud 'Hear, Hear' from Premier Sir John Forrest.[10] The member from the goldfields FCB Vosper did not oppose the venture, but felt the House should reflect on the fact that in Western Australia people knew, 'nothing about the justice or injustice of the war'. This observation led to the following exchange with Forrest.

The Premier: We do not want to know.
Vosper: We know nothing about the merits of the case.
The Premier: You are arguing that we do not belong to the
             Empire.[11]

Forrest was soon to become the defence minister in the first federal government.

Other senior figures in Australian politics showed a similar insouciance in relation to the politics associated with the war. The prominent lawyer-politician and first federal prime minister, Edmund Barton led the debate about involvement in South

Africa in the New South Wales parliament. He argued that if the empire had decided on a course of action it was the obligation of the colonies to respect and follow. It was not necessary for them to be consulted. They could rely on the wisdom and intelligence of the British authorities particularly because they were 'of the same blood' and 'belong to the same race'. It was as if Barton, like Forrest, did not want to know. As long as Australia was part of the empire,

> when our empire is at war with any other power whatever, it becomes our turn to declare the motto, 'The empire right or wrong.' That, at any rate, is the view which I have a right to express.[12]

Similar statements of blind loyalty were made in the other colonial parliaments.

Dissent and disquiet

The opponents of military involvement were as much of a minority in 1899 as they had been in New South Wales fourteen years before and their arguments would have been familiar to anyone who had listened to that debate. The Labor members of the Queensland parliament were particularly hostile to the venture. Anderson Dawson denounced the 'war craze, this thirst for blood, the jingoistic spirit'. His colleagues insisted that Queensland had no interest in the impending war, and knew almost nothing about it. Henry Turley blamed the government for 'forcing themselves into a quarrel with which they have almost nothing to do'.[13] There was a sense that the venture represented a radical change in the external relations of the colony, although this was a contested claim as shown in exchanges between JC Stewart, the member for Rockhampton North and several ministers:

Stewart:	He [the premier] has altered the foreign policy of this colony.
Secretary for Railways:	We have no foreign policy here.
Stewart:	This colony and Australia generally has had a foreign policy. The foreign policy of this colony hitherto has been one of non-interference in matters outside the colony.
The Treasurer:	You are quite wrong.
Stewart:	Our foreign policy hitherto has been one of absolute non-interference in the quarrels of the Empire.[14]

Concerns about the precedent of engagement continued to agitate many critics of the militant turn. William Kidston asked the members of the government whether Queenslanders were to understand that this engagement marked a radical change in the colony's foreign policy and inaugurated a new era in relations with the Imperial government and,

> whether we are to understand that every time after this when Great Britain is engaged in a war anywhere throughout the whole world, that a contingent of armed men from Queensland will be sent to take part in that war; and if it does not involve that, who are to be the judges as to what are the right times to send contingents to help the Mother Country in her hour of need, and what are the wrong times?

If a future government declined to be involved would that not be, in effect, a censure of the Imperial authorities? It would subject a dissenting premier to the charge of disloyalty. To accept the present engagement, therefore, opened 'the flood gates very wide indeed'. Kidston wondered whether the premier had considered the 'far reaching consequences of this proposed action'.[15]

The commitment to South Africa met the most serious opposition in the South Australian parliament and only passed the Upper House by one vote. WA Robinson asked why the colony's soldiers should be expected to 'butcher those with whom they have no quarrel and whom they knew nothing about'. EL Batchelor warned about future commitments. 'Would the colony not have to keep this game up?' he wanted to know.[16] It was a question more often asked in Adelaide in 1899 than in any other city. Thomas Price enquired:

> What did this new departure which was proposed mean? It meant that we were laying down the principle that in future we were preparing to enter into England's wars, and to assist her with troops. Having done so once, we would be expected to do so again and again. It was a dangerous precedent for United Australia to create.[17]

Perhaps the single most important parliamentary critic of the South African involvement was the Victorian lawyer, Henry Bourne Higgins, who opposed the measure in both the Victorian and federal parliaments. He was particularly concerned about the one-sided and distorted news received in Australia via the Imperial news services. He objected to both the war itself and to Australia's involvement and he was particularly censorious of the large number of his parliamentary colleagues who were willing to acquiesce in Imperial policy without question, to say as Barton did, that Australia should support the empire right or wrong. Addressing his Victorian colleagues he declared:

> Several honourable members have said that we should not
> enquire too closely into the justice of the quarrel. That is
> what I object to. I say that we have no right whatever to
> enter into any war, or to spend a penny on any war, unless
> we do enter into the justice of it. It seems to me to shock all
> conscience for us to venture to go into war with a light heart
> and without inquiring closely into the justice of it.[18]

Higgins's scruples were not widely shared in Australia. Numerous observers noted that there was far less dissent about the war in the colonies than in Britain itself. The most prominent critic of the war was the professor of history at Sydney University, George Arnold Wood, whose views were very similar to, and were informed by, those of the English intellectual dissenters. But few other prominent people joined his lonely crusade. In a telling remark Alfred Deakin dismissed Wood's opinions as, 'not an Australian growth'. The English-born and educated professor had brought his ideas with him when he migrated and he would 'take them away again'.[19]

The morality of intervention

The decision to go to war was much easier taken if one could leave the political, legal and moral responsibility to the British leaders. The complexity of international conflict could be reduced to a few simple prescriptions. Australia was there out of loyalty to the Queen and gratitude to the Motherland. It had gone to lend a hand. No immediate political objective could be used to assess either the morality or the utility of the engagement. There was very little suggestion in the Australian parliaments, as there certainly was in Britain, that the involvement was undertaken to improve the lot of the Africans or the Indians in the Boer Republics. There was an appealing disingenuousness in the assumed innocence of the engagement. And if the reason why could be left to the Imperial leaders so could the moral opprobrium of the last brutal years of the war with the burning of farms and the imprisonment of women and children in what turned out to be death camps. There was great reluctance in Australia to accept any responsibility for what were, in modern terms, war crimes. Once again that could be left to the British. Anything else would spoil the home-coming of war-torn warriors.

There was little post-war debate about the wisdom of the engagement or any assessment of what, if anything, Australia had got out of the war. What, after all, had Australia gained at the cost of six hundred dead? As on so many occasions the bravery and sacrifice of the troops took the place of hard headed assessment of what they had actually achieved for Australia. To ask hard questions about the war was to diminish the service and show disrespect for heroes. It was allowing politics to intrude onto hallowed ground which was beyond the reach of calculation. But heroism aside the war ended badly and in Britain the wartime Conservative government fell and was then defeated in an electoral landslide in 1906. In South Africa the Boers gained control of the new republic in 1910 and the three generals Louis Botha, Jan Smuts and James Hertzog led the country for thirty-eight years. Britain came out of the war isolated with much diminished prestige and little to show for the vast expenditure.

The one question which greatly disturbed the Australians was the subsequent employment of Chinese labourers in the gold mines of the Rand. This occasioned a long and angry debate in the federal parliament in 1905, with fierce condemnation of Britain's betrayal of the white race. The small band of dissenters had reason to feel vindicated in their often lonely, sometimes beleaguered, stand. Perhaps more than anything else their fear about the inevitability of involvement in future Imperial wars was fully justified. If Australia had committed itself to a minor war against small farmer republics how could it avoid engagement in a future conflict with one or more of the great European powers?

Strategic anxieties

The Boer War had a dramatic impact on British diplomatic and strategic thinking. Her military forces had been put under great stress and alarm spread about the fitness of the nation. The European powers all had huge conscript armies. Demands for conscription in Britain grew stronger after humiliations on the veldt, but traditional resistance to a standing army prevailed. Consequently military planners looked covetously at the potential military manpower in Australia, Canada and New Zealand. The colonial troops had proved their value in South Africa, dispelling high level doubt about their reliability and discipline. The British planners hoped to ease two perceived strategic problems by the use of colonial troops. In the immediate aftermath of the Boer War the fear was that Russia, pushing through Afghanistan, would threaten India. By 1906 the focus was on the threat of German hegemony on the continent. Both scenarios highlighted Britain's lack of trained military manpower. In official circles there was no doubt that in the event of war the Australians would be there and this was the almost universal expectation in Australia itself. But promises of timely succour did not meet the needs of strategic planning. What the British wanted was a well trained expeditionary force of known size and established logistics over which they could assume command whenever they pleased. They wanted to be able to send this force anywhere that strategic logic demanded. It was an ambitious plan, but the British believed it was in the long-term interest of the Commonwealth, even if the Australians were slow to appreciate the point.

The leaders of the new federation were clear about two things when they thought about their fledgling army. They were determined to avoid all suggestion of the common European link between the officer corps and the aristocracy. They universally eschewed the idea of what they called a military caste and its association with epaulettes, spurs, sabres and social condescension. They wanted an army principally made up of part-time soldiers and came to favour the Swiss model of a trained citizenry. They did not follow through and adopt the Swiss commitment to neutrality and independence. But the logical corollary of a citizen army was that the entire focus of training and equipment was on home defence. This was continually frustrating for the British authorities and for the permanent senior military officers in Australia who were usually English and whose true allegiance was always open to question.

Yellow peril

But the Russo–Japanese war of 1905–06 had a bigger impact on Australia than the Boer War. The astonishing Japanese victory over one of the great European powers reverberated around the world. Australian leaders felt the shockwaves more than most. They became alarmed about the threat from the north. Prevailing ideas predisposed them to assuming both Japanese interest in and cupidity towards an underpopulated continent. Schooled in the ideas of Social Darwinism they assumed that nations were fated to be locked in a struggle for existence. Australians popularly assumed that race conflict loomed as a future certainty. And they thought, too, that population pressure would drive the Japanese in Australia's direction. The White Australia Policy was both essential for the future, but also a likely cause of provocation and future tension.

The relationship between these obsessive ideas and objective reality were tenuous at best, but they were shared by many of the leading figures of Australian political and cultural life. Senator George Pearce, federal defence minister for many years between 1908 and 1921, believed that 'earth hunger in eastern nations' would lead them to 'pick a quarrel with Australia for the purpose of securing these valuable and only partially populated lands'.[20] The journalist and future war historian, CEW Bean, wrote an article in 1907 for the English journal the *Spectator* explaining Australia's strong commitment to 'racial exclusiveness'. He began by asserting a commonplace belief at the time: the White and Oriental races could not live together in Australia. That being so the 'probability of an Oriental invasion, peaceful or warlike' was enormous and justified urgent action. Believing that a 'fierce racial war' was inevitable, the Australians were determined to fight it at any cost, but the future stance of Britain was seen as uncertain.[21] The defence minister at the time of Bean's article, TT Ewing, was haunted by similar apocalyptic spectres, warning his parliamentary colleagues:

Every sane man in Australia knows that, if this country is
to remain the home of the white man, it must be held, not

by the power of Australia alone, but by the might of the white man in all parts of the world. In years to come, it will take the white man all he knows to hold New Zealand and Australia. Therefore, we must not break the link which binds us to our fellow countrymen in other parts of the world. By consideration, generosity, and a broad appreciation of our responsibilities and dangers, we must seek to knit together the white man of this and other lands in preparation for that last deadly conflict which will assuredly come upon Australia.[22]

Despite the power of their convictions, Australian leaders knew almost nothing about the country they assumed had designs upon their territory. The American scholar and university president, DS Jordan, visited Australia in 1907 and gave a series of illustrated lectures on Japan in which he tried to 'dispel the dense ignorance regarding that country'. He came to appreciate how widely spread was the view that Japan was planning to annex the tropical north. 'Gross misapprehension as to the people of Japan as a whole' and the purposes of their government 'prevailed everywhere and it was considered a matter of patriotism to believe them'. Jordan observed that the situation was being exploited by 'interested militarists' to promote compulsory training and increase defence spending.[23] Australian leaders carried their ignorance with them into international forums. At the 1911 Imperial Conference in London, the prime minister, Andrew Fisher responded to the views of both British and Canadian delegations that Japan presented no threat with a truly extraordinary outburst. Speaking from what he claimed was his, 'own experience twenty five years ago', he declared that the Japanese were at that time 'very glad to come down to our country, and they came in very large numbers', and it had been necessary to solicit the support of Britain to 'prevent them establishing themselves seriously in the country'.[24] Fisher may have had some personal experience years before, but it had little relevance to the matter in hand. He was clearly referring to Chinese not Japanese migration.

Two of Fisher's colleagues, Senator Pearce and the external affairs minister EL Batchelor, returned from the London conference via Japan. Their visit passed unnoticed but when they returned to Australia they reported they had met with no hostility. This observation perplexed the Japanese. The English language newspaper the *Japan Times* wondered why they expected that there would be any.[25] Japan had little interest in Australia and the official stance was that migration should only be encouraged into countries where their expatriates would not meet racial prejudice and consequent loss of face. There is no doubt the Japanese would have been willing to enter into an official understanding with Australia about migration similar to the so-called Gentlemen's Agreements negotiated with Canada and the United States, the conditions of which set a quota on migrants which were scrupulously adhered to. The British foreign secretary Sir Edward Grey reminded the Australians at the 1911 conference about the agreement with Canada and indicated that the Japanese had never raised the question of immigration with the Imperial government.

Imperial cynicism

Australia's widely canvassed fear of Japan was both a problem and an opportunity for Britain. She entered into an alliance with Japan in 1902 and it was an important and valued connection which was maintained until after World War 1.

Their own official strategic assessment of 1906 saw little possible threat to Australia and no likelihood of invasion. But by 1911 the message of antipodean security was no longer useful to the British and while preparing for the Imperial Conference, the Chief of the Imperial General Staff, General Sir William Nicholson, had become aware of how frightened the Australians were about Japan. He had consulted the Australian Agents General in London and had been told that the 'possibility of a Japanese invasion of the northern territory of Australia with a view to settlement was viewed with much anxiety'. Such an illusion was just too useful to dispel. So Nicholson was opposed to allowing the Australians to see the relevant memorandum as being 'likely to discourage them' in the measures they were now taking to develop their military forces. He continued his observation:

> If, as stated in the memorandum, Australia could in no
> circumstances be exposed to the danger of attack more
> formidable than could be delivered by a small raiding force,
> it could not be maintained that a large military force was
> essential to the security of Australia.[26]

The cynical manipulation of Australia's phobia about Japan was maintained right up to the outbreak of war. Early in 1914 the Inspector General of Overseas Forces, and soon to be commander of the Anzac campaign, General Sir Ian Hamilton, toured Australia and New Zealand. He fully exploited local fear about Japan both in public and in private as he reported in letters written to his friend Prime Minister H Asquith. It was important correspondence and needs to be quoted at length:

I had fully meant when I came out here to urge upon the Commonwealth the importance of having some small section of their army earmarked, in peace, for expeditionary Imperial service. But I see now I could defeat my own object and weaken the effect of the whole of the rest of my report were I to touch on that string. The whole vital force of the country i.e. the rank and file of its people, are standing firm together against any such proposition. Play the tune an Australian army for Australia, and they dance to any extent. Not otherwise. Australia – not Empire – is then the string we must harp on. That is to say, we must encourage them to do what they will do willingly and lavishly, namely pay up for safeguarding a White Australia from the cursed Jap. Then, when the time comes, and when we are fighting for our lives in India or elsewhere, I for one am confident that the whole military force of Australia will be freely at our disposal. But tell the Australian that he must contribute to a force which may have to fight outside the areas washed by the Pacific, and he at once begins to talk tribute.

Therefore I am acting on the principle of encouraging Australia to make her land forces as efficient and strong as possible to meet dangers threatening their hearths and homes and am talking as little about overseas Imperial needs as possible.[27]

Hamilton's audacious cynicism graphically illustrated two things about Australia on the eve of World War 1. She was burdened with an unrealistic fear of Japan and an exaggerated sense of dependence on Britain. But what the British realised, and the Australians didn't, was that by 1914 they needed Australia more than the new federation needed the empire. Sir Charles Lucas was one of the most experienced and able officials in the

Colonial Office and he knew Australia well. In a book published in 1912 he observed that if England was to 'hold her own as a nation; she must keep the Dominions with her'. In fact, he declared,

> it is probably true to say, though it may not be generally admitted, that each succeeding year adds conspicuously to the population of the young peoples of the world, whether inside or outside the British Empire. The value of the Dominions to England increases in much greater proportion than the value of England to the Dominions, because each year each Dominion comes nearer the time when it can defend itself, and each year England without the Dominions, tends to be more outdistanced in population and home resources than some of her foreign competitors.[28]

Prophesies vindicated

Lucas was visiting Australia when war broke out in 1914. He would have been delighted at Australia's response. Even though the country was in the middle of an election campaign, an immediate commitment of a twenty thousand-strong expeditionary force was made and it was to be sent, it was assumed, to Europe. All the expenditure of the previous five years, the establishing of ordnance factories, the compulsory training, the education of a cadre of officers at Duntroon, had been undertaken with a hostile Japan in mind and fears of looming racial conflict in the Pacific. Fratricidal warfare between the most advanced members of the white race was not what had been expected.

The long argument between those who wanted Australian armed forces to be used only for the defence of the continent itself and their opponents who hoped for the creation of an expeditionary force to be deployed wherever it was required overseas by the Imperial government had been decisively settled. While discussing his engagement in the frantic preparations to dispatch the force Senator ED Millen, who had been defence minister until the election of 1914, told his colleagues that it was obvious,

> that our defence scheme has been designed solely for the purpose of resisting an invasion of Australia. All the preparation has been made in contemplation of some raiding party coming here, and we have ... made no preparation for service abroad. The result is that when this call came there had to be a great deal of improvisation. There was not a single man, officer, uniform, cartridge, or gun earmarked for anything but service within Australia.[29]

Australia's leaders dutifully accepted the Imperial argument that the country's fate would be determined in north-western Europe. Defence minister G Pearce argued that the country was 'as much involved in war with Germany as if Germany were invading our shores'. He completely identified with the British point of view. A few dissenters took up the arguments of the critics of 1885 and 1899. In the Senate the Queensland Labor member, J Stewart, argued, much as he had done in the Queensland parliament in 1899, that in such uncertain times it would be wise to keep at home 'our best men for defence purposes'. If the danger to Australia was so great, it was folly to send both men and equipment to the other side of the world. He believed that Australia should confine itself to the defence of the continent. Other senators interjected, saying Australia was already at war, with Pearce declaring: 'We are being attacked in Europe at present.' Millen argued that the country was, 'fighting today for our national existence', because there was no portion of the empire which was 'in greater danger than this Australia of ours'.[30]

Many of the colonial Cassandras who had spoken out against the involvement in the Sudan and South Africa were dead in 1914, had left public life or had changed their minds. In the loyalist mood of the time their foreboding had largely been forgotten. But we might at this point recall the burden of their concern. Britain, they were convinced, was a source, not of security, but of danger. With interests all over the world it was certain at some point that Australia would be pulled into one of her wars. The reverse situation where Britain would enter a war on behalf of Australia was unlikely to be realised. Australia's geographical isolation was an advantage not a liability. Unlike Britain she had no obvious enemies and the enormous effort needed to mount a sea-born attack made invasion unlikely. Her disengagement from the world in the nineteenth century, her neutrality as some termed it, should be maintained. Commitment to Britain's wars in Africa would establish a dangerous precedent and make future ventures more rather than less likely. Britain would expect to be able to call on Australia again and would likely make plans assuming that outcome. The prospect of being drawn into a European war chilled many of the dissenters. They correctly foresaw what a catastrophic outcome it would be for Australia, undertaken not from inescapable necessity or immediate danger of attack, but from choice and a failure to distinguish between Australian and Imperial interests. HB Higgins warned, with fearful prescience, in 1899, that war implied 'unlimited liability'.[31] The first twenty thousand were only the start. How could Australia limit the commitment once so deeply involved? By war's end over three hundred and thirty thousand had served; sixty thousand had been killed and one hundred and fifty thousand wounded. Higgins himself had lost his much loved, only son.

Were the dissenters right? Were Australia's engagements in the Sudan and South Africa mistakes? Did they establish a precedent so vice-like, that it was inescapable? The radical scholar JA Hobson observed, in 1901, that the Imperial leaders, while referring to the Australian involvement in the war, boasted that 'this confederacy in bloodshed has annealed the colonies to the mother country'.[32] Such speculation must inevitably address the question of the Anzac landing. The venture had all the characteristics the dissenters had feared. Instead of keeping the armed forces in Australia for use against threats to the security of the continent, or simply for national development, the leaders of 1914 had accepted the strategic logic of the expeditionary force with its assumption that the best defence was to engage the putative enemy half a world away. They had also taken on board the assumption that Australia's safety lay in an almost complete identification with British policies and strategic interests. It was not so much an alliance as a familial embrace. They still spoke without any hint of embarrassment of the 'Mother Country'. But it was not a simple question of whether or not Australia would be caught up in the war, but rather the nature of the engagement. Australia was probably legally at war from the moment of the relevant declarations. But it was not inevitable that Australia would send so many young men to fight in Europe. In their war planning the British had considered the possibility of limiting the engagement of the Australian forces to areas outside the continent. This was not their preferred position, but they may have accepted such a situation if Australia had demanded it. The country was committed in advance to war, but not to the massive involvement beyond our shores. The Anzac venture was, then, not just a flawed campaign, both strategically and tactically, but a tragic and wholly avoidable Australian disaster.

How does this relate to the way the Anzac campaign is remembered and commemorated? Can we, in all seriousness and solemnity, continue to assert that the landing made Australia a nation? In his recent book, *Gallipoli*, Robin Pryor argued that the time for sentimentalising the landing has 'long passed'.[33] It was a brave call because it is so difficult even at this distance to admit that so many young Australians died needlessly and that their sacrifice produced so little benefit. And that leads inevitably to a consideration of the way the whole engagement in World War 1 is assessed. If the war itself was, as prominent contemporary scholars now insist, 'the greatest error of modern history'[34] or 'a tragic and unnecessary conflict'[35], it must have been even more so for a small country like Australia on the far side of the world. The nation gave so much in order to maintain the balance of power in Europe and yet many of the countries most directly involved – Norway, Sweden, Denmark, Switzerland, Holland and Spain – remained out of the conflict. Even Britain's ancient ally Portugal maintained her neutrality until 1917. It is a thought which haunts me every time I see a war memorial in a small country town and am reminded again of the terrible loss of life in World War 1. They are not just monuments to Australia's loss, but to the folly of a generation of leaders who thought that loyalty was a sufficient reason to go to war and believed in the empire, right or wrong. But they may also remind us of those colonial politicians, the Cassandras, who warned that the militant turn had opened the floodgates to future tragedy and the threat of a descent into an 'abyss of misery and wretchedness'.

—3—

Whatever happened to the anti-war movement?

Carina Donaldson and Marilyn Lake

> HUGHIE COOK: Why remember it? Why go on and on remembering it? Oh yeah, 'that's war' … Well, war's such a dirty thing I'd have thought as soon as it's over you'd want to forget it, be ashamed, as human beings, ashamed you ever had to take part in it.
>
> ALF COOK: Ashamed? Ashamed? To fight for your country?
>
> Alan Seymour, *The One Day of the Year* in *Three Australian Plays*, Penguin, Ringwood, 1963, p 27

It was with such provocative dialogue that Alan Seymour's play *The One Day of the Year* erupted onto the Australian scene in 1960. Its pointed criticism of the militaristic and antediluvian values of the Anzac legend, as well as its condemnation of the uncouthness of the annual celebration of Anzac Day, fiercely divided an Australian nation in the midst of rapid social and cultural change. Banned at the first Adelaide Arts Festival in 1960 on the grounds of its perceived insensitivity to returned servicemen and with bomb threats levelled at theatrical companies daring to produce it, *The One Day of the Year* incited one of the most significant literary controversies to that date in Australia. When Seymour came to revise the script for a new production in the 1980s he decided to delete the critical anti-war passage quoted above.

Although provocative in its attack on the annual ritual of Anzac Day, *The One Day of the Year* was not the total aberration it might now seem. That war was 'a dirty thing' and mass slaughter an 'obscenity' were the messages that Australian peace groups, whose members bore witness to the unprecedented loss of life in World War 1, had been propagating ever since. Thus did a young Victorian Methodist minister, Hubert Palmer Phillips, who had campaigned for conscription, later reflect on his change of heart when he encountered returned soldiers in the 1920s: 'when the boys began to come home and talk to me of the horrors and obscenities of modern war, my whole outlook changed and before long I had become a convinced pacifist'.[1] As did many thousands of other Australians.

The long anti-war movement

Just as the Anzac legend was born in an attempt to comprehend and transcend the terrible loss of life in World War 1, so too was the widespread anti-war movement. Indeed revulsion against war and the rejection of long-held ideas that a nation's worth must be proven through blood sacrifice were among the most significant outcomes of Australian participation in World

War 1. As Eleanor Moore, who became leader of the Women's International League for Peace and Freedom wrote of the effect of the study circles she joined: 'Our hearts had told us the war business was all wrong; now we began to see it with understanding also.'[2]

The view propagated by Anzac mythology that World War 1 was a creative experience for Australia in that it made us a nation was an obscene idea for many in the 1920s and 1930s. Few families were untouched by the huge toll of death and injury. More than sixty thousand had died and many thousands more would die from their wounds in the years to come. In 1924, the Victorian Methodist Conference established a special committee to inculcate hatred for war and the following year ruled that war was 'un-Christian'. At the same time, the newly elected Victorian education minister instructed his department to ban all articles extolling wars, battles and military heroes from their publications and school textbooks and to replace them with publications that promoted peace and internationalism. A 'No More War' demonstration sponsored by the Society of Friends in 1926 was attended by fifteen other organisations, including the Socialist Party and the Women's Central Committee of the Victorian branch of the Australian Labor Party. Even New South Wales' governor, Sir Philip Game, used the occasion of an unveiling of a war memorial in 1930 to state: 'None of us can say that the world is better for the Great War.'[3]

With so many dead and wounded talk of 'the great blood bath' pervaded post-war life. The searing critiques of the English poets, Siegfried Sassoon, Wilfred Owen and Robert Graves spoke to Australian as well as English audiences and the sense of disillusionment with modern civilisation was profound. Anger increased with the large number of exposés of the profits generated by the armaments industry: titles included *Patriotism Ltd: An Exposure of the War Machine*, *The Bloody Traffic*, *Death and Profits*, *Iron, Blood and Profits* and *Merchants of Death: A Study of the International Armaments Industry*. The Australian authorities worried about the long-term effects of the anti-war mood. Nettie Palmer thought that Australian publishers discouraged authors from writing anti-war books, while the Returned Sailors' and Soldiers' Imperial League of Australia (hereafter abbreviated to RSL) called for all war books to be censored by the official historian. In the 1920s and 1930s 'war books' were usually 'anti-war books'.[4] The New South Wales and South Australian governments tried to ban *All Quiet on the Western Front*, with its depiction of the shared humanity of German soldiers and it was not alone in attracting the attention of censors.

Despite the heroic account of Australia's engagement in the war by official historian CEW Bean, many private memoirs and letters – including those written by returned soldiers – expressed anger and disillusionment with a post-war experience that didn't seem to justify the terrible cost of war. George Johnston captured the mood in his classic novel *My Brother Jack*:

> Much bitterness had built up out of the war and by the time I was about thirteen all the retuned soldiers we knew had come to see the whole conflict as a monument of disorganisation and waste and political chicanery. They had had their years in the trenches but the world of mufti to which they had returned had hardly become a fit place for heroes. Life, in their own words, was a 'fair cow'.[5]

Many returned soldiers were cynical about the cant and hypocrisy surrounding their new-found status as Anzac heroes. As unemployment worsened in the 1920s and 1930s and soldier settlers were forced off their farms, many returned men felt duped and betrayed. 'After wasting 10 years of the best part of my life on a proposition which the Commission admits is hopeless from a wheat growing point of view I do not want to be forced out with a debt chasing me', wrote one returned soldier. 'Simply because I was an 18 year old hero in the war and upon my return had sufficient faith in human nature to believe the lies told of the Mallee ...'

Another wondered whether the Closer Settlement Board took pleasure from causing 'fresh distress to a miserable wretch of a Returned man who served with honour in Gallipoli and Flanders – smallest man in the 8th Batt. In action at the original landing at Anzac, and right onwards until crippled ... at Pozieres.' Another reminded the government of its promises:

> I suppose this is a sample 'of a country fit for men to live in'. I gave up a good position and was prepared to put up with a lot of inconvenience when I decided to take up an allotment in answer to the Govt's cry of 'Go on the land' but by heavens I was and am not prepared to be fooled with ... apparently a man's letters are not even worth acknowledgment nowadays, but if there happened to be another war and he was foolish enough to write and offer his services I suppose they would send a motor car or aeroplane for him.[6]

Publicly feted as heroes, many returned soldiers clearly felt neither adequately compensated nor at all consoled by Anzac mythology. Their anger and sense of betrayal fuelled anti-war sentiment between the wars. It remains a sharp rebuke to the de-politicised sentimentality that has informed so much of the recent writing and political speech-making about Anzac.

The advent of the Depression with its further degradations intensified many people's disenchantment with an old order in which capitalism and war seemed mutually implicated. Peace groups proliferated in the 1920s and 1930s as political leaders and ordinary citizens, men and women, young and old vowed 'never again'. As Lord Robert Cecil, founder of the League of Nations Union (LNU) and patron of the worldwide disarmament movement noted, the 'horror of war' was an 'argument for peace'. The World Disarmament Movement joined numerous groups including the Women's International League for Peace and Freedom, the University of Melbourne Peace Group, the Student Christian Movement, the Melbourne Peace Society, the Movement Against War and Fascism and the LNU, in swelling the demand for an end to war. Together they secured one hundred and eighteen thousand Australian signatures for the Declaration on World Disarmament in 1931, one of the largest petitions in the world, which was presented to the Australian prime minister amidst 'a wave of emotion'.[7]

The LNU enjoyed an astonishing standing among people on both sides of politics, in universities, churches and women's groups. Members included prominent Australians such as scientist David Stead, Professor George Arnold Wood and feminist Rose Scott in New South Wales; HB Higgins, Meredith Atkinson, Professor Sir Harrison Moore in Victoria and West Australians, Professor Fred Alexander, Dr Roberta Jull, delegate to the League of Nations in 1929 and Bessie Rischbieth, president of the Australian Federation of Women Voters and delegate to the League of Nations in 1935. Most were idealists and internationalists, fearful of the 'moral abyss' into which the world had lurched and critical of the role of nationalist pride and racial prejudice in perpetuating it.

Feminists were deeply committed to international activism, spending much time and money travelling to participate in overseas conferences and join organisations, such as the International Council of Women, the Woman's Christian Temperance Union and the Pan-Pacific Women's Congress. 'The Women's Movement', explained Bessie Rischbieth, 'views men and women not so much as members of a particular race or nation, but as members of the human family, each with a special vocation in the world to perform in the cause of human progress'.[8] The League of Nations encouraged idealists to explore new ways of living as citizens of the world. Anzac Day provided an occasion to commemorate and grieve for those who died in the war, but it was unthinkable that it should be set aside for the celebration of the nation. Indeed in the 1920s Armistice Day became the occasion for well attended peace rallies.

Reaction against the war converted many leading Australians into convinced internationalists. Justifications of wartime losses with nationalistic appeals to the 'spirit of Anzac' or the 'birth of the nation' were denounced as dangerous folly. Only by thinking in terms of people's common humanity and shared sympathies would future wars be prevented. HB Higgins who had famously denounced Australia's support of Britain in the Boer War and reluctantly supported World War 1 was beset with recriminations and grief when his only child Mervyn enlisted and was killed: 'I have been condemned to hard labour for the rest of my life.' Higgins became an ardent supporter of the World Disarmament Movement and member of the LNU, hoping that international activism would be effective in preventing further waste of life. 'Even if the Germans were all criminals', he wrote to his American friend Felix Frankfurter, 'we have to live in the world with them ... Vengeance is a fruitless thing. I feel that the best vengeance my boy could hope for would be an integrated world, an organised humanity.'[9] Higgins became president of the Melbourne branch of the World Disarmament Movement formed on Armistice Day in 1928, which attracted one hundred and twelve affiliated organisations throughout Australia.

With the rise of Nazism and anti-Semitism in Europe in the 1930s and the international leadership against fascism offered by the Soviet Union, many in the peace movement followed the new direction provided by the Movement Against War and Fascism, with older-style peace workers joining forces with, but agonising over, the implications of the 'united front'. In 1935 the United Peace Council affiliates included the Australian Aborigines League, the Australian Church, the Teachers' Peace Movement, the Woman's Christian Temperance Union and the YMCA. The different strands of the peace movement came together in a peace march in Melbourne in 1936 described in the press as 'probably the strongest public peace demonstration yet organised in Melbourne and it gained strength as much from its representation as from its numbers'.[10]

The Australian Peace Congress in 1937 in Melbourne was attended by around four thousand people from diverse social and political backgrounds of all ages. Delegates registered to work with different 'Commissions'. 'Youth' was to the fore at this Congress with its own 'Commission' attended by four hundred delegates, who reported:

> The prospects of a worthwhile and useful living for the Youth
> of today depend for their fulfilment upon the progressive
> establishment of peace based on justice, freedom, economic
> security, co-operation and goodwill. We deny that war is
> inevitable and reject the fatalism and inaction fostered by
> such teaching.[11]

Self-consciously, those too young to serve in the last war called for a repudiation of old ways of thinking and insisted on their voice being heard in national policies that should work to prevent another war. While old men made the political and military decisions, it was the young who were expected to sacrifice their lives for them.

Youthful idealism survived the outbreak of World War 2, which was widely supported as a 'just war' – especially after Nazi Germany's invasion of the Soviet Union – and inspired visions for a new national and international world order and in Australia the project of 'post-war reconstruction'. With the new threat of nuclear war, however and the belligerent international relations fostered by the Cold War, activists once again formed peace councils and joined the international Campaign for Nuclear Disarmament. Some peace activists were Communists; others were labelled as such by the conservative political forces that ruled Australia in the 1950s, led by the Coalition government of Prime Minister Robert Menzies.

The most powerful lobby group in Australia

The RSL was a powerful voice in that decade, calling for national unity in the name of national security, lobbying hard to have the Communist Party banned even after the defeat of the referendum on the issue in 1951 and for compulsory military service to be re-introduced. In 1962 it distributed thirty thousand copies of a booklet entitled *Subversion: The RSL Case Against Communism in Australia*.[12] Later reflecting on its strident commitment to what he termed 'assertive Australian nationalism', Sir Albert Abbott, Queensland branch president, described the RSL as the 'the voice of stability in changing times'. While the tone of the RSL was sometimes harsh, Abbott said, 'sometimes harsh words were needed to protect and defend a principle or a belief dearly held'.[13] Although convinced of its special right to speak in the national interest, its chief business of winning improved war pensions and repatriation benefits for returned soldiers in fact confirmed its status as a special interest group.

The intolerance and vociferousness of the RSL provoked an increasing number of attacks from its critics, including the growing number of students attending universities, who included future historians, Geoff Serle, Ian Turner, Bob Gollan and Russel Ward, who would craft a version of Australian history with the civil and political values of egalitarianism, republicanism and socialism – not the spirit of Anzac – at its heart. In the 1950s, as in the 1930s, university students and their friends criticised war-mongering in the name of the future of young people, whose sense of separate identity was strengthened by the emergence of a perceived 'generation gap' between the young and older Australians. For these youthful rebels, freedom meant an escape from parental hypocrisy and they gave vent to their frustration and impatience in the rude tirades against authority that characterised student newspapers in the 1950s.

In the lead up to Anzac Day in 1958, Geoffrey Havers, a student at the University of Sydney, delivered an attack on what he called the 'yearly pageant of national necrophilia, which joins Australians in a day of morbid joy and unity'. Anzac Day, he charged, had become a national obsession: 'the Spaniards have bullfights, the English have soccer and the Queen, the Russians have tractors and the five year plan, the Americans have Hollywood and Americans'. He wondered if 'the men in the Australians units who landed at Gallipoli 43 years ago knew what they were starting … a festival of hero-adulation unequalled anywhere in the world':

> The words flow, the hymns are sung, the wreaths placed.
> The old women weep before the cenotaph, while the new
> generation of the militia finishes its marching and gets
> down to the serious business of pickling itself in alcohol and
> accosting prostitutes.
>
> The old generation of militia, not so very unlike their
> modern counterparts, ensconce themselves in the RSL clubs
> and also internally immerse themselves in alcohol.[14]

What seemed to puzzle Havers was the combination of hedonism and mourning, of cenotaphs and racecourses. But what gave meaning to the public ritual was the peculiar status of the returned serviceman in post-war Australia:

> Australians as a race seem to be intensely conscious of
> their armed services. Even thirteen years after the last great
> conflict, the Returned Serviceman has represented the
> epitome of Australianism. How often have we heard the
> statement that 'Australians are the best assault troops in
> the world' or 'We might not have had the parade-ground
> discipline of the other troops, but our battle discipline
> was much higher'. Do not Returned Servicemen get first
> preference in the ballots for farms, special rates from certain
> real estate agencies, and other less tangible but never-
> the-less equally telling advantages? Who will deny that a
> stranger wearing an RSL badge and walking into a group of
> Australian men is welcomed as a long lost brother?[15]

Those who believed that 'trained assassins are Australia's foremost export' comprised, he thought, the main supporters of Anzac Day. Other Australians enjoyed the holiday, but didn't really give a damn. They were hypocrites and simply took advantage of a day off work. The only people who won Havers' respect were the aging parents, but their mourning merely served as a reminder of the pointlessness of war, its 'sadness and horror and idiocy'. In sixty years time, there would be none left who grieved: 'Perhaps this will be the time to do away with Anzac Day.'[16]

Havers' article attracted immediate attention and was widely condemned for its insulting portrayal of returned soldiers as pickled in alcohol and accosting prostitutes. The federal president of the RSL condemned it as 'complete and utter filth'. The University of Sydney Senate summoned the editor of *Honi Soit*, David Solomon and demanded that the Student Representative Council discipline the paper, which it refused to do.[17] Freedom of expression was surely one of the Australian values that returned soldiers had fought to preserve. Gallipoli veteran WC Smith, who had heard about Havers' article on the radio, wrote to *Honi Soit*: 'I have nothing to do with Anzac Day. To me it is a glorification of war. There are many ex-servicemen who share my views. In my immediate vicinity there are three ex-AIF members ... none of us take part in Anzac Day celebrations'.[18]

The RSL noticed the combined indifference and hostility to Anzac Day and resolved to defend it. CW Joyce, NSW State Secretary of the RSL explained that the reason their magazine *Mufti* included so many articles promoting the observance of Anzac Day was because 'the Press so frequently and unremittingly puts the opposing view'.[19] In 1961, *Mufti* featured a double page spread called 'The story of Anzac – Foster the day and keep our national unity intact' arguing that Australia would lose its soul and character completely if national pride, gratitude and emotion became weaknesses to be ashamed of, and if youth gathered 'no obligation from the past'.[20] By rushing to the defence of Anzac Day, however, the RSL itself increasingly became the target of radical criticism for seeking to impose its outmoded views on the rest of society.

The attack on Anzac Day and the RSL continued in university newspapers. The new editor of *Honi Soit*, David Ferrero defined 'The spirit of Anzac' as 'one of the most pernicious which the human spirit possesses. The RSL calls it patriotism. Perhaps a better word would be jingoism – the same feeling that motivates Hitler's Germany and Tojo's Japan.' Condemning the 'annual ritual of national narcissism-cum-Bacchanalian revel' the editor took particular aim at the 'blood and thunder and syrupy sentimentalism of RSL propaganda'.[21] When an abbreviated version of 'The spirit of Anzac' was published in the University of Melbourne student newspaper, *Farrago*, the RSL denounced the editors as 'the scum of our so-called intelligentsia' and demanded that the students 'be taught a lesson'.[22]

The University Chancellor duly reprimanded the students for being 'wild, youthful, irresponsible and silly' – for behaving like students – and rebuked them for their 'disgraceful ingratitude', but subsequent correspondence in *Farrago* showed that there was considerable support for the editor's viewpoint. While some correspondents took him to task for 'the desecrating gripes, the gratuitous insults and offensive fulminations of a pack of student upstarts' and demanded they be punished for the 'sickening tirade of the most insulting type', others congratulated them for their defiance of tradition and applauded their honesty in uttering views many had held for years.[23]

Alan Seymour, a young ABC writer who had recently moved to Sydney from Perth, noted the controversy and saw in it the generational clash – and the clash of values – that would become the basis of his controversial play. He told a *Sun* journalist: 'Something was simmering in the young people I met.' Australia was in 'a transitional phase', he later recalled, 'and young Hughie sums up his generation's distaste for old customs and institutions'.[24] Anzac Day came to symbolise all that students wanted to change in society. Rather than feting the returned soldiers as heroes, students mocked them as relics from a past they wished to leave behind.

The One Day of the Year dramatised the widening gap between young university-educated Australians, such as Hughie Cook and older Australians such as his father Alf, a World War 2 veteran and a proud Australian, who champions the Anzac tradition as he asserts he is 'bloody Australian and will always stand up for bloody Australia'.[25] His son Hughie, on the other hand, is clever and cynical. The first in his family to attend university, his admiration for Australia's proud soldiering past has been corroded by his exposure to a campus atmosphere driven by the forces of modernity and change.

In the ensuing conflict between father and son, Hughie denounces Gallipoli as 'the biggest fiasco of the war' and 'an expensive shambles' that resulted in 'men wasting their lives'. The Anzac myth was simply a 'face saving device'. He tells his father: 'Every year you still march down that street with that stupid expression on your face you glorify the – bloody wastefulness of that day.' Together with his middle class girlfriend, Jan Castle, he produces an illustrated article for the university's student newspaper which draws attention to the uncouthness and bibulousness of Anzac Day, a day that now 'disgusts' him and makes him 'ashamed' to be an Australian. He tells his mother Dot:

We're sick of all the muck that's talked about on [Anzac Day] ... the great national day of honour, day of salute to the fallen ... It's just one long grog-up ... It's a lot of old has-beens getting into the RSL and saying 'Well, boys, you all know what we are here for, we're here to honour our mates that didn't come back'. And they all feel sad and have another six or seven beers.[26]

At the end of Act Two, a dishevelled and drunken Alf arrives home after an Anzac Day 'on the grog'. For Hughie, Alf's appearance confirms his contemptuous judgment of Anzac Day, but his attitude ignites a bitter family row that leads Alf to give his son a backhander. Alf responds with violence to his son's taunts, but the play doesn't go all Hughie's way: in the end there's a suggestion that there may be wisdom on both sides of the argument.

The choice of *The One Day of the Year* by the Adelaide Arts Festival's Drama Committee in 1960 as the Australian play with which to open the festival caused immediate protest by the festival's board of governors, which included prominent members of the local RSL, and it was banned before it could go into production. But immediately after the festival, Jean Marshall, director of the Adelaide Theatre Guild, chose to defy the conservative views of the 'Adelaide Establishment' and to stage *The One Day of the Year* at a small hall in suburban Adelaide. The production opened with a plain clothes police presence in the audience and outside the hall after they had received 'threats of a bomb or some other disturbance'.[27]

The first professional production of the play was performed to a full capacity audience at Sydney's Palace Theatre for three weeks in 1961. Seymour was pleased with the play's success and wrote a letter to the *Sydney Morning Herald* to emphasise people's positive responses: 'Night after night people poured backstage to congratulate the players. I received many letters from members of the public, including a most touching one from a Gallipoli veteran's widow, who was moved by the play.'[28] But one irate theatre-goer complained to the *Sydney Morning Herald* that *The One Day of the Year* was 'doomed even before it was written' because its theme – 'let's throw mud at Anzac Day' – 'insulted rather than wooed its intended audience.[29]

The Sydney season was followed by a Melbourne production by the Union Repertory Theatre Company at the Russell Street Theatre in Melbourne, which then toured regional Victoria, South Australia and Tasmania. In federal parliament, the minister for territories described the play's themes as 'subversive' and labelled Seymour a 'communist'.[30] Seymour meanwhile left for London, where *The One Day of the Year* opened at the Theatre Royal and received a standing ovation.[31] Seymour would live and work in exile for some thirty years, joining a wide range of cultural expatriates from Menzies' Australia.

Under the direction of Rod Kinnear and with John Sumner as producer, the Russell Street production was adapted for television and was named best television drama for 1962 at the *TV Week Logie Awards*. Such high profile acclaim led to the play's inclusion on Higher School Certificate booklists throughout Australia and for many years it was prescribed as a text for schoolchildren as an introduction to debates around Anzac Day. In 1966, it was taken to Tokyo for performance in an English speaking theatre that was filled to maximum capacity of six hundred for all eight performances. Sydney actor, Ben Gabriel, who played Hughie in the production, asserted that the play was an 'inspired choice' for Japan, despite the young student audience's lack of familiarity with the Anzac legend they 'identified strongly with the young people in the play. One young man said to me with great feeling, "I am Hughie Cook" and the girl with him added, "I am Hughie Cook – but different".'[32]

In Australia, even as the RSL called for national unity, its own interventions in political and social life had ever more divisive effects. Aware of its reputation for militarism and intolerance, the RSL attempted to craft a new public image more in harmony with a modern national identity as its membership steadily declined. From a high point of three hundred and sixty thousand in 1946, it had dropped to two hundred and forty-seven thousand by 1956. In 1961 *Mufti* advised returned soldiers in a special article on public relations: 'If you are addressing a school' on Anzac Day not to 'glorify war' or 'overdo talk of another war' and to 'include the women', because 'the whole nation was at war, not merely those in the fighting forces'.[33] In 1964, Dr Jim Cairns, member of the House of Representatives for Yarra, told a cheering crowd of his supporters at the Richmond Town Hall that there was a 'lot of talk about threats to Australia and its way of life', but 'the real threat to freedom comes from the RSL and other reactionary organisations'.[34]

By the mid-1960s the RSL had formally dropped the 'Imperial' from its name and adopted the gender-neutral description of its membership – the Returned Services League – but by then satirists at O*z* magazine had identified a more general type of Australian in the character of Alf in *The One Day of the Year*. The racism and bigotry of 'Alfs', they thought, were a product of suburban consumerism and conformity that 'went along with beer, telly and the motor mower'.[35] The 'Alf movement aimed to convert you to a clean living, all-Australian, anti-erotic, healthy, mentally retarded citizen' and 'Eternal Vigilance' (the

RSL motto) was the method they employed to crush dissident minorities (including atheists and intellectuals).[36]

Anzac Day as day of protest

The critique of the RSL among university students that erupted into the public domain in 1958 was influential in shaping the larger critique of Anzac Day and the Vietnam War that developed later in the 1960s. On 25 April 1966 in Melbourne women from the anti-Vietnam War movement SOS (Save Our Sons) wore SOS sashes and carried posies with the words: 'Honour the Dead with Peace'. Protesters demonstrating against Australian involvement in the Vietnam War and the introduction of conscription staged anti-war demonstrations, sit-ins and teach-ins at universities throughout the country and used Anzac Day as an occasion to make their point. In 1968 Adelaide members of the Campaign for Vietnam Protest carried a placard 'Lest we forget the Vietnamese' and the following Anzac Day, the radical group Students for a Democratic Society lay a wreath at the Cenotaph in Sydney with placards that expressed their sympathy for the victims of Australian soldiers: 'Lest We Forget people who face war, oppression and injustice.'[37] Anzac Day services had once again been transformed into battlegrounds.[38]

The burning of Draft Cards became an emblematic gesture of defiance by 'conscientious objectors', who were forced into hiding, while those arrested and imprisoned became martyrs sacrificing themselves for the pacifist cause. As relatively uncensored media coverage of the Vietnam War flooded Australian homes with images of the barbarous realities of the war, including street executions, children with napalm burns and news of the Mai Lai massacre, the traditionally distinct lines between 'war hero' and 'war criminal' became blurred. Australians were forced to confront a horrific and futile war whose realities stood in stark contrast to the heroism and nobility of battlefield sacrifice talked about on Anzac Day.

Criticisms of Anzac Day as a drunken orgy and Gallipoli as an expensive shambles prepared the ground for the larger anti-war movement of the 1960s and 1970s, which was eventually successful in ending conscription and Australian participation in the Vietnam War. Returning Vietnam veterans then felt doubly defeated: by the military enemy on the battlefield and domestic opponents of the war on the home front, whose triumph was symbolised by the election of the radical Whitlam government, in which Dr Jim Cairns, leader of the Moratorium marches – protest marches intended to stop the war – served as deputy prime minister.

The contest over Anzac Day and then Vietnam was part of a larger cultural struggle over the sort of society Australia should become. For the moment a new nationalism flourished that celebrated a progressive, urban, culturally innovative nation committed to the goals of sexual and racial equality, an Australia that was forward looking and multicultural, rather than locked into the British traditions of its past. In 1973 the Australian Labor Party even discussed at its annual conference the desirability of dropping Anzac Day in its current form and replacing it with a day of peace.[39] Participation in Anzac Day marches fell away during this period. In 1969 the *Age* reported that Anzac Day had met a 'cool reception' with observers almost outnumbering participants; young people in particular were 'noticeably sparse'.[40] An accompanying photograph showed them to be elsewhere, gathered down the road at the Forum Theatre to see a film featuring the popular rock group 'The Monkees'.

Women had been active in the anti-Vietnam protests from the 1960s, an experience which propelled many into the burgeoning women's liberation movement.[41] From the 1970s feminists used Anzac Day as an occasion for protest against sexual violence and the rape of women in war. The Women Against Rape collective in Canberra together with similar groups in Melbourne and Sydney were particularly active in protests and laying wreaths 'in memory of all women of all countries in all wars' on Anzac Day in the early 1980s, drawing on international feminist discourse to critique the exclusions and repressions of masculine national tradition.[42]

Rehabilitation of the Anzac as tragic hero

Even as anti-war protest surged, new social histories of Australian soldiers at war were being written, such as Bill Gammage's *The Broken Years* (1974) and Patsy Adam-Smith's *Anzacs* (1978) which began to shape a new narrative in which the young soldiers themselves became the focus. Cast as the innocent victims of war, as in Peter Weir's film *Gallipoli*, they became the embodiment of youthful sacrifice. As historian Jenny McLeod has argued, whereas the close association of the RSL with the Anzac tradition had alienated progressive historians, once the RSL was increasingly marginalised in the telling of the Anzac story, historians were free to 'describe it anew'.[43]

Thus was the ground prepared for dissolving the distinction between attitudes to the soldiers and the wars in which they fought. This was also deemed necessary to the political imperative of providing appropriate recognition and restitution to Vietnam veterans, many of whom felt bitterly exiled from the

Anzac legend and the tradition of the soldier's heroic return. Increasingly all 'Anzacs' were cast as national heroes as debate about the justice or legitimacy of the wars in which they fought faded away. The new emphasis on the youth and innocence of soldiers – and their status as victims – was reinforced as children, grandchildren and great-grandchildren of the fallen and the aged were permitted to join Anzac Day marches. Far from being Anzac's fiercest critics, the young had now emerged, according to the *Sun* newspaper in 1981, as 'the new Anzacs'.[44] Distanced by decades from the horror of World War 1, the new recruits to Anzac were free to celebrate 'the Anzac spirit'.

Rewriting *The One Day of the Year*

These shifting attitudes to Anzac were vividly reflected in the changes Alan Seymour made to his play in anticipation of a new production in the mid-1980s, revisions that not only caused it to lose its sting, but also its audience. In the revised version of *The One Day of the Year* it was no longer the ordinary returned soldier whom the play's youthful protagonists blame for the excesses of militarism, but the 'top brass' who ran the RSL. In the new version, Hughie and Jan realise that in their 'smart little expose' they had been 'attacking the wrong people'. One of Hughie's original, most critical, speeches ('Why go on remembering it? … war's such a dirty thing …') had been entirely cut from the script. In a new speech, Jan shifts the blame. The enemy is redefined in class and political terms, with a focus on the RSL:

My father is a very big wheel in those Returned Servicemen's outfits. And he's a successful businessman, he is listened to.

He and ... all the top brass up there in our very attractive
little neck of the woods ... They tell their members what to
support, what to veto as unpatriotic ... [they] have so much
power – so much bloody power – and do not like it to be
challenged in any way. The rank and file – like your father
– turn up faithfully to meetings, to the ceremonies, but who
arranges it all, makes sure it's perpetuated year after year?
The big men, nice, discreet, behind the scenes men like my
father who really do believe – because of their money and
position – really believe they've a God-given right to say
what's good for us all.[45]

The criticism of Anzac Day no longer targeted the 'screaming
tribe of great, stupid, drunken no hopers' who marched every
year, but the 'puffed up, self-important bastards' who coordi-
nated it.[46] By the last Act in the revised version of *The One
Day of the Year*, the 'big men' in 'Returned Servicemen's outfits'
have been revealed as the enemy 'behind the scenes', while the
'ordinary little man' – the ordinary Anzac – is redeemed and
rehabilitated. In a 2003 interview Alan Seymour had become
distinctly defensive about the anti-war message of his original
play: 'The text emphatically does NOT attack or criticise the
Australian troops who fought so bravely at Gallipoli.'[47]

In the later version of *The One Day of the Year* the blame
for the excesses of Anzac Day had been shifted on to the RSL
which had been discredited through its reactionary, partisan
and sectional politics. It had become an organisation that could
be criticised and lampooned with impunity. Clearly Anzac was
being tarnished through its association with sectional interests
and divisive attitudes. For the mystique of Anzac to survive it
had to be rescued from its original custodians to become the

property of the nation-state. The RSL had to be sacrificed for the greater good of the Anzac tradition, which would henceforth be conceptualised as both the legacy and heritage of young Australians, who would be entrusted with the revival of Anzac into the new millennium. In the 1990s, the long-established and once powerful RSL would be effectively displaced and disempowered as the federal government, through its agencies the Australian War Memorial and the Department of Veterans' Affairs assumed national custodianship of the 'spirit of Anzac'.

—4—

Why do we get so emotional about Anzac?

Joy Damousi

'Calm down all emotional responders ... [and]
consider ways we can identify and shape our
collective consciousness about our nation, its past and
its future ... Perspective, and consideration of views,
not hotheaded defensive reactions, please ...'

Gail, *Age* blog, 23 April 2009

Gallipoli is 'part of our national consciousness, it's part of our national psyche, it's part of our national identity', said Kevin Rudd defiantly, in November 2008, 'and, I for one, as Prime Minister of this country, am absolutely proud of it'. He was responding to the view of former Labor prime minister, Paul Keating, that the 'truth' of Gallipoli was 'shocking for us': 'Dragged into service by the imperial government in an ill-conceived and poorly executed campaign, we were cut to ribbons and dispatched – and none of it in the defence of Australia'. The idea that 'the nation was born again or even was redeemed there was an utter and complete nonsense'.[1]

As we have seen, few historical myths continue to arouse such a deep and passionate response in Australian contemporary life as Anzac. Debate over the most appropriate form of remembrance is ongoing, while many people object to it being debated at all. Some argue that any questioning is profoundly disrespectful of those who gave their lives. Others believe that without such a debate, Australian national identity will be framed by an unquestioning acceptance of a national war story that is exclusive rather than inclusive and based on a narrow representation of Australian achievement. Its chief proponents, including leading voices in the daily press, argue that 'Anzac Day is a crucible of shared sentiments, it is about the values Australians would want to exhibit in adversity and about aspirations they hold for their peace and freedom'.[2] The *Age* editorial on 25 April 2009, however, expressed a bold note of dissent: Anzac Day was 'a day for the nation but was not our national day'.[3]

This chapter looks at how this debate draws out many emotional responses that seem to defy historical or political engagement. As a result, we have a mythic tale that doesn't allow – indeed resists – an engagement with some of the key historical and political issues in understanding the genesis of the commemoration and its subsequent ramifications. Yet it is the role of the historian to provide analysis and explanation. History is a critical and intellectual practice. Historians also have an ethical responsibility to engage with a range of perspectives that do not simplify but complicate the story of Gallipoli and the memory of war. Family members of those who served identify with battles and battlefields in particular ways, while journalists and political commentators have different interests. In recent times, some historical writing itself has begun to reflect the sentimental turn evident in wider community responses to war commemoration. Mark McKenna and Stuart Ward recently pointed to the tendency of historians to become complicit in the sentimentalising of war while failing to analyse the production of these emotions.[4]

What do these public emotional responses suggest about the way we commemorate Anzac Day? Expression of strong emotion is a way to avoid discussion and circumvent debate. Most significantly, such reactions de-politicise war commemoration by reducing the event to an emotional story of sacrifice and service. In his Armistice Day address at the Australian War Memorial on 11 November 2004, Prime Minister John Howard rejoiced in the way that young people were 'seeing in the sacrifice of their fathers and grandfathers and great-grandfathers a wonderful Australian saga'.[5] With the actual wars receding into the background and young Australians relating to them through their grandfathers and great-grandfathers, sentimentality and nostalgia are perhaps now the prevailing modes of relating to Anzac Day. It is present in the responses of backpackers who travel to the battlefields, and who recall youthful loss and heroism on the beaches at Gallipoli with little apparent knowledge of the reasons the soldiers were sent there or the role they played in the events of the Great War.

The history of the response to Australia's involvement in overseas wars has clearly been characterised by deep emotions. Whether it be anger, revulsion, fear or patriotic enthusiasm, in commemoration and memorialisation, war has until recently attracted passionate engagement. As we have seen, earlier generations were disturbed by the destruction caused by war and questioned its purpose; they were angry with their elders for condemning young men to a futile war and the waste of lives. For those in the 1960s and 1970s, Australian engagement in the war in Vietnam became the rallying point of opposition against all the forces that conspired to send men to die in Vietnam and that led, also, to the systematic abuse and rape of women. A resistance to critical debate on this subject today – and indeed a hostile response to the suggestion of debate – represses alternative narratives about the meaning of war and what it means to be Australian. A critical examination of the costs and consequences of war, its horror and waste, the mistakes and massacres is resisted and repressed.

What has led to this shift in the late twentieth and early twenty-first centuries? One of the major changes is the merging of military and family history, in a way that encourages identification with our military past – with the experience of grandfathers and great-grandfathers – and a proud investment in that nationalist history. Those who speak from the perspective of a familial connection seem to claim a special authority to speak – sometimes as those who inherit the Anzac tradition. Even as World Wars 1 and 2 recede into the distance, the descendants of those who served necessarily multiply in numbers – the grandchildren of Vietnam veterans now attend university – and these proliferating family connections sustain the new wave of commemoration and national identification. Thus have discussions of Anzac, war and nation-building become increasingly devoid of historical analysis, yet it is analysis that is urgently needed to understand the emotional dynamics of the new wave of popular pride in the Anzac story. 'I've been to Gallipoli', reported one Aussie backpacker on the *Age* blog, 'and the sense of pride and spiritual emotion was enormous. It made me proud of our fallen [heroes].'

Should history get emotional?

Writing in 1935, the philosopher RG Collingwood reflected on whether emotions should be the stuff of history. He thought that history was an account of men's thought and rational life. 'Many human emotions', he reflects 'are certainly bound up with the spectacle of ... life in its vicissitudes ... but this is not history ... [T]he record of immediate experience with its flow of sensations and feelings, faithfully preserved in a diary or recalled in a memoir, is not history. At its best, it is poetry; at its worst, an obtrusive egotism; but history it can never be.'[6] In recent times Collingwood's view has been challenged, although many historians would still agree with him. Numerous historians continue to prioritise stories of rational decision-making and tend to see the play of emotions as irrelevant to historical inquiry, politics or culture. Since the 1980s however a new field of historiography and cultural analysis has opened up questions about the role of emotions in national and political life.[7]

Historians of the emotions have approached their subject in three ways. Firstly, by looking at historical attitudes towards emotions through popular advice literature relating to anger, violence or, for example, crying in public. Secondly, by providing grand narratives of the history of the West as a place of increasing emotional restraint: from the violent, barbaric and unashamed, even childlike, Middle Ages to the control, self-discipline and repressions of modernity. Finally, historians have examined the process whereby emotions are shaped and managed though specific social discourses and vocabularies. The expression of emotions may be universal, but 'the ways those emotions are themselves elicited, felt and expressed depend on cultural norms as well as individual proclivities'.[8] The story of

Anzac joins individual sentiment to powerful narratives about nation and war promoted by government agencies and political leaders as we see in later chapters.

All three approaches to the history of emotions have been important in opening up discussion on emotions and the past, but it would seem especially relevant here to see emotions as key dynamics in cultural and political life, informing political mobilisations and movements for cultural change. In my own work on mourning, memory and the two world wars, and using psychoanalysis as a cultural theory, I pointed to the ways in which grief was politicised, as the suffering of marginalised groups became a force that animated their political claims.[9] In these studies, I looked at the fathers, mothers and widows who lost their sons and husbands in war and reflected on the ways their collective group memory of historical loss and suffering mobilised them to not only claim compensation for their losses, but also to demand cultural and political recognition of their grief. For them, this history of loss was fundamental to who they were as they attempted to win acknowledgment of their private loss. Emotions then can be seen as central to the social, political and cultural process itself.

As chapter two states, although the colonial expeditions to the South African war were enthusiastically supported, they were also resisted, notably by Liberal intellectuals HB Higgins and George Arnold Wood. Some radical nationalists – such as those associated with the *Bulletin* magazine – opposed the war upon their fellow white men in the Boer Republics of the Transvaal and the Orange Free State. Others queried why – especially at the beginning of Australia's life as an independent Commonwealth – Australians should be part of a war in which they had no say.

World War 1 created emotional divisions on the home front as well as destruction in the trenches. Violence erupted in the fiery conscription debates of 1916–17 with speakers pulled from platforms and physically assaulted. The anti-conscription pamphlet, produced by the Women's Peace Army called 'The Blood Vote' appealed to mothers of the nation to resist sending their sons to kill other mothers' darling boys. At the same time, pro-conscription propaganda appealed to the need to stop the murderous Hun raping women and slaughtering children. The ongoing conflict between returned soldiers, socialists, women's activists and peace activists was marked by verbal and physical violence. During the years between the wars, different groups ranging from the Returned Sailors' Soldiers' and Airmen's Imperial League of Australia to widows' organisations raised their voices in an attempt to be heard by the authorities, making emotional arguments about their special status deriving from their experience of loss. Some returned soldiers, impatient with the compromises of civilian life, also joined aggressive right-wing political movements such as the New Guard.

Australian involvement in World War 2 generally attracted strong and widespread support; divisions in Australian society were not as pronounced as during World War 1. Different forms of violence erupted on the home front with public brawling, for example, between Australian and American soldiers based in Australia which left some combatants dead. Australian involvement in the Vietnam War incited strong opposition from the late 1960s that often focussed on the annual commemoration of Anzac Day. The feminist critique of rape in war – expressed in confronting public demonstrations – provoked angry responses in turn from the guardians of the Anzac tradition in the Returned Services League (RSL).

Interestingly Australian historiography on Anzac over the last decades has itself been marked by a discernible shift from studies of the political aspects of the history of Australians at war, which dominated narratives from the 1970s to the 1990s, to a recent sentimentalising of wartime experience. Works with titles such as *The Cost of War* and *Loyalty and Disloyalty: Social Conflict on the Queensland Homefront, 1914–18* have been replaced by studies such as *Returning to Gallipoli* and *Shattered Anzacs* which adopt a markedly more sentimental perspective on the impact of war and its history and which have enjoyed publication subsidies from the Department of Veterans' Affairs (DVA) and the Australian War Memorial. The focus of earlier studies was on how war created new tensions and conflicts in society and exacerbated old ones, such as those between men and women. Instead of unifying the nation, the effects of most wars had been to divide it. The new status given to returned men after World War 1 and the assertive conservative political stand of their official organisation, the Returned Sailors' and Soldiers' Imperial League of Australia (RSSILA), often added to these divisions. Bill Gammage's *The Broken Years* and the film *Gallipoli* set the new trend in their focus on soldiers as the innocent victims of war. This theme has continued in recent scholarship, especially historians documenting the emotional response to the battlefield pilgrimage.[10] As Ken Inglis noted in the *Age* in 2005, the rhetoric of the Anzac, whether in political speeches or academic histories, now drew more and more on 'the vocabulary of sacrifice and victimhood'.[11]

Some interesting questions arise from an examination of the history of the emotional response to Australian involvement in war, in particular with regard to the ways emotions have animated, and been manipulated by, larger political movements.

There are also questions about the role of renewed national pride – at a time of international insecurity – in inspiring more widespread identification with the celebrations on Anzac Day. Alan Davies has noted that 'political movements intensify, hoard, refine and bind anger and hatred ... Ideology binds anger by proving that hostility serves a purpose – and can be, and is being, deployed according to some systematic and efficacious strategy'.[12] Anzac ideology serves to disarm the critics of Australian participation in war and of the militarisation of Australian history. Supporters of Anzac Day become hostile to critics; they lash out at doubters as disloyal and un-Australian.

These emotional responses were evident in the *Age* online discussion that followed the publication of Marilyn Lake's article on the 'Myth of Anzac' last April (see the introduction). Indeed it is arguable that the ascendancy of the 'blog' forum has encouraged a new form of public discourse, which is emotional, spontaneous, polemical, anonymous and uncensored. Significantly, in the debate on the 'Myth of Anzac' many bloggers introduced themselves by establishing their personal family connection to the Anzac tradition, which implied a special right to speak: 'My family has been military every generation for over 200 years, and fought in a multitude of wars.' Another contributor who thought that it was important to know more history than that of Gallipoli nevertheless pointed out: 'for the record, 3 of my ancestors fought in the Great War, all three in France, two never returned. My grandfather was in Darwin and Papua New Guinea.' Prime Minister Howard exemplified this approach – the fact that both his grandfather and father had served in World Wars 1 and 2 – to demonstrate his own authentic relationship to the Anzac tradition.

Military history and family history

The connection between military history and family history is promoted in schools by DVA curriculum materials and pedagogical strategies and genealogical resources, including Nominal Rolls, provided by DVA and the Australian War Memorial (see chapter six). This link between family and military history has shaped a new sense of pride in the role of military sacrifice in shaping the nation, and in encouraging families to locate themselves in the national story. The emotional tie that connects military history and family history is encouraged by the use of the blog which presents debate in a particular form, creates a community of participants who generally use incomplete identifications and adopt a polemical style and provide immediate responses. As a medium for debate and exchange of ideas, it operates in different ways from nineteenth and twentieth century modes of debate about war, which involved face-to-face encounters or arguments in print, though as we have seen these debates could be just as emotional.

In the *Age* online discussion, Ian thus expressed pride in his family history of military service. He had a father who served in World War 1, a brother in World War 2, and a grandfather in the Boer War. Their 'sacrifices' had ensured 'our freedom today'. Sean made a similar point:

> My ancestors also fought in all wars since the Boer War and all served, including women family members in whatever capacity they could. They and their comrades DESERVE honouring and remembering ... ANZAC Day is glorious and at once sad, terrifying ... inspiring and part of our history. That it commemorates sacrifice and not revolution, so much the better!

Sinistra also emphasised the familial investment in the national story:

> Five men from my family went to Gallipoli – 2 died on the
> beaches, 1 went on to Africa and died there, 2 went on to
> France and both survived. Neither was ever truly whole ...
> and would rarely speak of those days. And while neither ever
> went to a dawn service, both would go to the pub, and raise
> a glass for those who would not again ...
>
> It is not about honouring the guns ... It's about honouring
> the guts behind them ... and thanking them ...

'I am a war widow', wrote one aggrieved woman, 'and I deeply resent the comments made in this newspaper, after seeing the trauma my husband went through, memories too painful to talk about ... This is what the first Anzacs did, they heard the cry for help, saw the injustice been dealt and answered the call. They did not stop to query the rights and wrongs of it, they acted, if they hadn't would we enjoy the freedom we are so lucky to have today?' Interestingly, Deputy Prime Minister Peter Costello cast the Anzacs' actions in remarkably similar terms in a radio interview with Neil Mitchell on 3AW on 25 April 2003:

> There are problems in the world today just as there were
> in 1915. You can't turn your back on them ... and young
> Australians, even today, are serving in the Middle East
> because they want to make a difference ... And you think
> back how their grandfathers and great grandfathers would
> have felt the same in 1915.

All generations of Australians from World War 1 through to Iraq, he said, had 'answered the call'.

Having family connections – fathers and grandfathers who answered the call – did not always lead however to uncritical support of Anzac Day flag-waving as Troy noted:

As an ex-member of the Australian Defence Force and having members of my family having served in both WW1 and WW2, I attended ANZAC day ceremonies without fail. That was until I attended a ceremony at the Shrine of Remembrance at the height of John Howard's reign, and in my view, the height of the trumped up mythology for the purpose of social identity and political gain.

During that ceremony many stories and speeches were given, each of which related to Gallipoli. The service then concluded. What left me quite disturbed is that at the time we had defence force servicemen in harm's way in Iraq, Afghanistan and East Timor and not a single mention was made of them. Not to mention the countless Vietnam and Korean War vets present. I have not attended a dawn ceremony since.

Australia needs to drop the sentimental garbage that ANZAC day has become. The soldiers of Gallipoli must be honoured, however, they are not apostles to be given religious reverence.

Daniel suggested that a history of family sacrifice in war should lead to protest rather than celebration:

I'm surprised why relatives of people who served in World War I aren't angry about it. I would be angry if my grandfather died at Gallipoli. He would have been enlisted against his will, sent in without adequate strategy and resources against a heavily armed opponent who had a superior tactical position defending the cove. They were doomed from the start ... LEST WE FORGET is a good motto, we should never forget how stupid it was to have all that unnecessary death and destruction.

And Chris had learnt a critical attitude to war from his father:

My grandfather was an ANZAC; my father and both his brothers fought in WWII. None of them ever attended an ANZAC service and none of them ever went back to an RSL club after the first visit. The only thing my father ever told me about the war was that he would spend the rest of his life trying to forget what he experienced.

Significantly, the right to dissent from Anzac mythology and celebration was also grounded in and justified by a history of family engagement in war:

My grandfather fought in WWII. He steadfastly refused to attend an Anzac day event for the rest of his life. He felt that it glorified killing, revelled in death and perpetuated hatred.

So much of the online discussion of the 'Myth of Anzac' was characterised by what one participant called 'raw emotion' that calls were made for more rational and historically informed debate. All the 'emotional responders' were urged to 'calm down'. Warwick called for attention to the 'facts', but still felt obliged to point to his own family's tradition of military service:

It would be great if we could deal with facts and not get so emotional about things such as Gallipoli without knowing what really happened. People die in wars sometimes for noble causes and some less noble. I think there is a point in mourning the loss of life in all wars, but at the same time not brandishing people as heroes unless the cause was really a good one to fight for. There is definitely a lot of mythology around Gallipoli and it is really difficult to have an honest discussion about the subject. My great grandfather died in World War 1 leaving a wife and 5 children. He had already gone to the Boer war. I believe this was a waste of life and that it would have been more noble of him to stay home. World War 1 was so tragic in so many ways and in the end caused the problems that led to World War 2. It would have been great to have heroes of diplomacy and peace at this time.

Another correspondent also believed the emotional response obscured the facts of history which were many and various:

Some people just miss the point and use raw emotion rather than a clear head to formulate their answers. No one has an issue with honouring those who served and died at Gallipoli. The issue is that Gallipoli is always championed as a point in history where our nation was born/came of age. I have never been able to understand this ... Gallipoli is hardly relevant for the development of this nation at all. We are where we are today because of a whole host of events that have happened over the years, and as time marches on the importance of Gallipoli only becomes less than it ever was. I mean federation in 1901, the rolling back of the white Australia policy, women's and aboriginal rights gained in the 1960s, the great migrations in the 1950s and 60s have all had a far bigger impact than Gallipoli. I would put the constitutional crisis of 1975 above Gallipoli ...

Disturbed at the flow of 'raw emotion', one contributor suggested that schoolchildren should be better educated to become critical readers and even more unusually, thought that academics and teachers had a key role to play in this:

> If there is a fault with Australia's education system, as suggested by some, it lies in its apparent failure to teach so many how to read critically. Questioning the cultural primacy of the ANZAC myth is neither traitorous nor disrespectful to the dead. One of the key roles of academics is to raise important questions, no matter how uncomfortable that might be.

Wes considered that raising such questions with a view to 'moving on' was in the current circumstances 'daring':

> If only we as a nation could truly move beyond the glorification of war. We all grieve the loss of so many in such atrocious circumstances. Hopefully we will one day move our focus more onto more positive and non-violent themes that seek to build tolerance and equality.

As the blog response indicates, many base their right to speak on their personal connection to Anzac through family, even if very distant and tenuous.

No more bunfights

Prime Minister Kevin Rudd thinks that to move forward we must learn from the past, but his history lessons are selective. When greeting soldiers returning from Iraq, he declared that he did not want to politicise their homecoming, or the war, as other generations had done, especially during the Vietnam War. 'The searing lesson from Vietnam', claimed Rudd, was 'never put our troops in the middle of a political bunfight. They respond to the direction of the democratically elected government of the day.'[13] Anzacs needed to be protected from political controversy. The lesson to be learned from the 1960s was not that our participation in the war in Vietnam was a ghastly mistake or that the introduction of conscription was unjust, but that anti-war protesters had caused embarrassment. To criticise our engagement in the war in Iraq would be to subject our returned soldiers to another 'political bunfight'.

In encouraging Australians' personal identification with our long history of fighting in overseas wars, the myth of Anzac has worked to discourage the kind of historical and political analysis that might just lead to more bunfights – or even worse – outright opposition to our participation in war. Joined now in celebration of the tradition that in Howard's words has 'shaped the character and destiny of this country more than any other tradition or influence', prime ministers Rudd and Howard are able to 'collectively rejoice in the growing embrace of that tradition'.[14] Once an occasion for personal mourning, for the expression of grief, regret and remorse about the loss of life and casualties of war, Anzac Day has been transformed during the last decade under the political leadership of prime ministers Howard and Rudd into a festival of national pride and collective rejoicing.

— 5 —

Anzac Day: How did it become Australia's national day?

Mark McKenna

'To Die for his Country was so dear but his Young
Life was Dearer.'

Epitaph on the gravestone of Lance Corporal
ST Bormann, 24th Australian Infantry, killed at Lone
Pine, Gallipoli Peninsula, 29 November 1915, aged
twenty-three

On 25 April 1916, at the first commemoration of Anzac Day, the New South Wales education director, Peter Board, described the 'national sacrifice' Australian soldiers had made 'in the interests of an Imperial cause'. At Gallipoli, he exclaimed, 'history and Australia's history were fused, and fused at white heat. Never again can the history of this continent of ours stand detached from World history. Its voice must be heard in the Councils of the Empire, because its men and its women have fought and died in an Empire struggle.' The Imperial struggle of Gallipoli is just one aspect of the Anzac legend that contemporary Australians have since learnt to forget. In 2010, our image of the Anzacs is a far cry from the hundreds of Gallipoli veterans who 'played two-up in the main streets of Sydney', 'danced, sang war-time songs, staged mock marches and directed traffic', on Anzac Day 1938. We have also forgotten the large numbers of men in the 1920s and 1930s, who returned from Gallipoli and suffered mental breakdown, died prematurely, or committed suicide; men who, as historian, Joan Beaumont recognised, saw 'little to celebrate' in Anzac Day. Nor do we see the men who boasted of the numbers of Turks they killed, or the men, overcome by the fear of death, who could not bring themselves to fight and deserted, or the men who came back home to find themselves unemployed and argued against the erection of Melbourne's Shrine of Remembrance in the late 1920s, because they believed that the monument glorified war. Like all national myths, the myth of the Anzac simplifies the past. We see the Anzacs as we need to see them: an army of innocent, brave young men who were willing to sacrifice their lives so that we might 'live in freedom'.[1]

In the early twenty-first century, Australians have embraced the Anzac legend as their most powerful myth of nationhood. Mourning the loss of life in the Victorian bushfires in early 2009, Prime Minister Kevin Rudd compared the firefighters who stood at 'the gates of hell', to the Anzacs in their 'slouch hats', as if any story of courage and loss must now be placed in 'the Anzac tradition' before national mourning can truly occur. After the criticism of Anzac Day that surfaced in the 1950s increased with the staging of *The One Day of the Year*, and intensified in the context of the anti-war movement of the 1960s and 1970s, the myth of Anzac has now been refurbished. We hear constant discussion of the 'resurgence' of Anzac Day and the 'timeless' Anzac tradition. But how do we explain the newfound enthusiasm for Anzac Day? And is this change a reconnection to the past or a fundamentally new form of commemoration?[2]

Over the last decade, analysis of the 'resurgence' has presented a now familiar train of explanations for Australians' rush to embrace the Anzac story. In *Sacred Places*, historian Ken Inglis led the way, pinpointing the crucial turning point as the late 1980s and early 1990s, when Anzac Day attendances began to rise steeply, followed shortly afterwards, in 1990, on the seventy-fifth anniversary of Anzac Day, when Bob Hawke became the first Australian prime minister to preside over the Dawn Service at Anzac Cove, after which the numbers of pilgrims visiting Gallipoli each Anzac Day rose sharply. The arguments put forward by Inglis have become the most commonly accepted explanations: the 'surge' of interest in family history that encourages Australians to pursue the fate of relatives who served in war, the steady demise of ex-servicemen and women, which has only made it easier for recent generations to commemorate war in their own image, and the urgent need for a 'civil religion' in a 'post-Christian society that no longer delivers ancient certainties to young people who are in search of nourishment for the spirit'. Removed from the experience of self-sacrifice, contemporary Australians are humbled, 'even awe-struck' by the 'supreme sacrifice' made by the generation of 1915. Each explanation contains important insights, but they offer only part of the answer. The 'resurgence' of Anzac Day, which stands at the vanguard of a new wave of patriotism in twenty-first century Australia, emerged out of the politics of nationalism in the 1980s. In order to understand why 25 April has become holier than 25 December in the Australian calendar, we have to look beyond the changing patterns of commemoration of Anzac Day itself, and examine the wider historical context in which the Anzac revolution occurred.[3]

The government-led campaigns designed to inculcate a deeper national attachment to Australia Day, which had been such a hallmark of national politics in the 1970s, continued with even more urgency in the 1980s. There was little choice. The bicentenary of European settlement at Sydney Cove (26 January 1788) was fast approaching. In 1980, the Fraser government established the Australian Bicentennial Authority, the statutory authority presiding over the official programme of events. Over the next eight years, millions of taxpayers' dollars were poured into a raft of government initiatives designed to instil greater national pride in the Australian people, ultimately culminating in the 'celebration of a nation' on 26 January 1988. Long before the celebrations were underway, opinion leaders noted the manifest failure of earlier attempts to whip up enthusiasm for Australia Day. Significantly, many of these remarks were made in a comparative context, contrasting the lacklustre response to 26 January with the authenticity of Australia's only 'true national day': 25 April. The comments of Vernon Wilcox, ex-serviceman and former Victorian attorney-general, were typical:

Genuine efforts have been made with Australia Day, but it seems hard to make it mean anything special – other than to clearly mark the end of the holiday season. Australia Day. What does it celebrate? I wonder how many Australians know that it relates to Governor Phillip and Sydney Cove on 26th January 1788? Many nations have national days. America has its Fourth of July, France has its Bastille Day, and anyone who has been in Paris on that day could not fail to commemorate it. Most countries have a national day and many of them have their origin in some heroic struggle. We have a ready-made national day if we want to use it. Anzac

Day – change its name to Australia Day if you wish, or Australia Anzac Day, or Anzac Australia Day.[4]

Wilcox's call for the authorities to rally around Anzac Day, and his hankering for a history of 'heroic' struggle, echoed the views of the *Australian* on 23 April 1980: Anzac Day was 'the one day of the year … when the whole nation knows what it is celebrating'. The nation could only be born and fused through the loss of sacrificial blood. Compared to Anzac Day, Australia Day was like a nativity play without the Christ-child. There was no grand design, no saviour, and no future martyrs to worship.

By the early 1980s, it was clear that Anzac Day was a more popular proposition as a national day than Australia Day. Over the course of the decade, as preparations for the bicentennial celebrations gathered apace, other difficulties surrounding 26 January emerged, difficulties which had surfaced as early as the Cook bicentenary in 1970, but which would now put an end to any hope of a united and cohesive national narrative being constructed around Australia Day. The dilemma was expressed succinctly in a slogan formulated by the Aboriginal protest movement: 'White Australia has a Black History'.[5]

As the bicentenary drew closer, the impact of the new critical histories of the last two decades, combined with the example set by the politics of the American civil rights movement, fed into an increasingly diverse and vocal movement of Aboriginal resistance. The memory of the Day of Mourning protest organised by William Cooper, Jack Patten and William Ferguson on the occasion of the sesquicentenary in 1938 was another source of inspiration. Even before the bicentenary, from the moment Aboriginal men and women, led by Kath Walker, donned mock, blood-stained headbands at La Perouse in 1970, and declared a Day of Mourning in opposition to the Cook bicentenary, the knowledge of the history of Aboriginal dispossession continually undermined national days of celebration grounded in the history of British settlement. By the mid-1980s, politicians and bureaucrats were struggling to find a way to 'celebrate' 26 January 1988. The media overflowed with reports of an increasingly polarised debate, which can now be recognised as the first stirrings of the History Wars of the last two decades. As the *Sydney Morning Herald* noted on 19 January 1988, 'scarcely a day of the Bicentenary has passed when issues involving Aborigines and their "Year of Mourning" protests have not featured prominently'. The media reported the prevailing Aboriginal response to the bicentenary. The twenty-sixth of January was not 'Australia' Day; it was 'Invasion Day', a 'Day of Mourning', a day that ushered in the dispossession of the 'First Australians'. How could this possibly be a cause for 'celebration'?

Large sections of the non-Aboriginal population were persuaded. Feature articles discussed 'white guilt' and 'national shame', while editorials spoke of the 'dilemma' posed by the coming two hundredth anniversary of first settlement. Conservative intellectuals and interest groups began to respond angrily to suggestions that Australia's 'British heritage' could not be commemorated positively. Unable to find a way through the competing voices, the Hawke government refused to support the First Fleet re-enactment, siding instead with the 'Tall Ships', a multi-cultural theme which would eventually see so many ships in Sydney Harbour on 26 January 1988, that no one could be sure exactly what was being 'celebrated'. As 'the First Fleet' entered the harbour, flying the Coca-Cola Flag, Aboriginal and non-Aboriginal protesters marched from Redfern to Circular Quay under 'Invasion Day Banners'. Looking back on the year's celebrations, the *Sydney Morning Herald* described what it saw as an 'ideological vacuum' at the heart of the bicentenary. The old problems remained. Australia Day, traditionally a holiday for both body and mind, despite all government-led attempts to give it serious purpose, was now beset with a far more intractable problem: entrenched Indigenous opposition. Throughout the 1980s, as Australia Day became a lightning rod for historical and political disputes, Anzac Day came to be seen as a less complicated and less divisive alternative.[6]

As early as 1980, eager to promote 'a feeling of nationalism', the *Australian* newspaper wondered if there might be grounds for changing 'the method of celebrating Anzac Day'. One year later, it was even more certain that Australia Day was a 'fizzer'. '[Should we] give up trying to make Australia Day our national day in favour of Anzac Day? 'The time has come', insisted the Anzac editorial in 1981, 'to look seriously at accepting it as such and proclaiming it as Australia Day ... just as the French celebrate Bastille Day, also based on a day of war [sic]'.[7] By decade's end, the *Australian's* call for Anzac Day to be recast as a more explicitly national day was well underway; the 'one day of the year', no longer an object of derision, was slowly beginning to secure a new role in Australian civic culture.

Writers, filmmakers and journalists performed narrative surgery on the Imperial history of 25 April 1915, casting it as a 'uniquely Australian' story in which a fledgling nation's innocent youth *fell* like sacrificial lambs. For decades following 1915, the Imperial context of Anzac Day had been fundamental to the rituals and meaning of 25 April; newspapers, for example, commonly placed the king's or queen's message on the front page. The day was linked inextricably with Australia's military contribution to the British empire. By the 1980s, the Queen's message, which is still sent every 25 April, had disappeared entirely from the front pages. Due to the success of Peter Weir's *Gallipoli* (1981), which drew on Bill Gammage's *The Broken Years* (1974), the 'Anzacs' came to be seen as the victims of British incompetence and condescension. Bruce Beresford's *Breaker Morant* (1980), and Simon Wincer's *The Lighthorsemen* (1987), reflected a similar emphasis. Once the venerable core of Anzac Day rituals, by the 1980s, the British had become 'the bad guys', reduced to the stereotype of the pompous Pom – hedgehog-moustached officers who spoke in plummy accents and held nothing but contempt for uncouth Australians – the perfect antidote to the problem of Anzac's Imperial past. In popular culture, Anzac Day was slowly being reinvented as an exclusively Australian odyssey.[8]

Anzac Day's demise had been prophesied since the 1970s. But Australians were now also solving this problem by replacing the dying diggers with new, more youthful marchers: their children and grandchildren, Vietnam veterans, now welcomed back as Anzacs after their allegedly poor treatment in the 1960s and '70s, women, and immigrants who had fought for foreign armies, including the Turks, who first led an Anzac Day march in Canberra, in 1974.

The political push for a more inclusive Anzac commemoration was not without resistance. In 1982, the Gay Ex-servicemen's Association publicised its intention to a lay a wreath at Melbourne's Shrine of Remembrance, and placed an advertisement calling on all gay ex-servicemen to meet in Carlton on Anzac Day. Bruce Ruxton, president of the Victorian Returned Services League (RSL), was adamant such people would not be allowed to participate. 'I don't know where all these queers and poofters have come from. I don't remember a single poofter from World War Two'. Ruxton promised to prevent any 'kissing' or other deplorable acts at Melbourne's Shrine of Remembrance, linking the gay campaign to that of 'Women against Rape', a group that staged a six hundred-strong protest at the Australian War Memorial, in Canberra on Anzac Day in 1981, and were responsible for some of the most disruptive demonstrations around the country in the 1980s. They have 'lesbian connotations', said Ruxton, 'I've seen the proof, it's all part of a deliberate campaign by some people in this country to destroy Anzac Day.' Far from destroying Anzac Day, the public forgetting of Anzac's Imperial origins, together with the broadening participation in the march, was in fact laying the foundations for a fundamentally new type of national day. The rising sense of Gallipoli as the only true crucible of national identity was helping to wrest control of the commemorative rituals of Anzac Day away from its traditional custodians such as the RSL which, as chapter three shows, was increasingly seen as an ageing, controversial, out of touch lobby group.

As the old men in medals decreased in number, and the generation gap became less pronounced, the common criticisms of 25 April that had emerged in the 1950s and 1960s were undermined. It seemed ridiculous to accuse young people of glorifying war. As journalist Tony Stephens remarked in 1988, 'the old divisions' were 'fading away': 'the critics have discovered respect for the men and women who went, not to glorify the barbarity but to honour old comrades'. 'This new understanding', Stephens thought, had 'been emerging for a decade or more'. It also represented a displacement of the fierce divisions over Australia Day in the lead up to the bicentenary. On 25 April 1990, the seventy-fifth anniversary of the Anzacs landing at Gallipoli, the connection between the failure of the bicentenary celebrations and the new embrace of Anzac Day was made abundantly clear.[9]

At Gallipoli, in his speech at the Ari Burnu cemetery, where one hundred and fifty-one Australians were buried, Prime Minister Bob Hawke told the audience that the hills around them had once 'rang' with the voices of the Anzacs; even more importantly, they 'ran with their blood'. In the 'exploits' of the Anzacs, he said, Australians were 'proud to identify the very character of our nation'. Speaking later to the media, Hawke observed that the pilgrimage made by so many Australians to Anzac Cove in 1990 represented 'the regeneration of the spirit of Anzac'. At the same time, his government decided to add the Australian War Memorial and Canberra's Anzac Parade to the National Heritage List. Newspapers carried photographs from the Dawn Service at Anzac Cove, showing 'the last' of the diggers, a seated line of frail, aged men, showered with medals. The *Sydney Morning Herald* reflected the view of the nation's major broadsheets: Anzac Day was becoming 'entrenched as our national day'. The critics had finally 'given up their bluster'. While Australia Day was plagued by a 'lack of national pride', Anzac Day was simply 'about being Australian'. Then, as if the nineteenth century struggles for responsible government and federation, and the decade of nation-building by Liberal and Labor governments that followed World War 1 did not exist, the editorial declared that the death of the Anzacs was 'the starting point of our nationhood ... the beginning of a separate identity from Britain that did not mature, perhaps, until we baulked at sending troops to Europe when Australia was under threat in 1941'. What's more, the Anzac spirit had

more to do with mateship and sacrifice than conquest and

power ... bloodlust was not the mark of the Anzacs ... the numerous diaries written on Gallipoli betray an absence of bloodlust that is hard to comprehend today ... the diggers were determined to prove that Australians were as brave or braver than men of any other nation.

The Anzacs were no longer the soldiers 'whose blood was up ... rushing northwards and eastwards, searching for fresh enemies to bayonet', as reported in 1915 by the British correspondent, Ellis Ashmead-Bartlett. Stripped of bloodlust, they were now sanctified as men who preferred to have a yarn with the Turks during ceasefires, crack jokes and swap cigarettes.

How different this was too, from the *Herald's* characterisation of the Anzacs at the beginning of World War 2, when a different historical context demanded an almost Homeric image of the Anzacs:

> These muscular, grim-faced veterans who had scaled the heights of Gallipoli exactly a quarter of a century ago, who later destroyed the Ottoman power and helped so effectively to turn the tide of war in France, symbolized the prowess of Australian armed forces and the indestructible strength of an Empire ... this offshoot of Britain in the South Seas has a fighting tradition which it will strive desperately to uphold. Despite the passing of the years, the grey hairs and the spectacles of middle age, these men had the cool, quiet confidence of seasoned soldiers who knew war and victory too ... the martial spirit of the Anzac still gleams and glows.[10]

There are few better examples of the way in which each generation moulds the Anzac legend for its own purposes: furious killers in 1915, cool and confident killers in 1940, and by 1990, brave boys loyal to their mates, whose virtues the nation might now emulate.

When Prime Minister Bob Hawke addressed a national television audience of millions in 1988, he could not bring himself to mention the dispossession of Aboriginal Australians. He spoke only of the need for a 'commitment to Australia' and of Australia's success story as a nation of immigrants. Delivered at the Sydney Opera House, only a stone's throw from where Arthur Phillip raised the Union Jack on 26 January 1788, the silences in Hawke's speech revealed the dilemma that had plagued the bicentenary celebrations since 1980. The history of Aboriginal dispossession, of which Phillip's landing was the opening act, undercut any attempt to present Australia Day as the rallying point for national pride. Eighteen months later, at Gallipoli, Hawke, like much of the nation's press, turned to the Anzac story with a sense of relief. After a decade of cultural and political division over 26 January, here at last, was a day that could be shaped into a true source of national communion. The blood spilt in the frontier wars, the taking of Aboriginal land without consent or compensation, the physical and cultural decline of Aboriginal communities, and the political demands of Aboriginal activists, none of these need haunt or spoil the commemoration of Anzac Day.[11]

Anzac Cove, not Sydney Cove, was where the right kind of Australian blood had been spilt. Hawke looked up at 'the steep cliffs' above 'the narrow beaches', and saw the metaphor of heroic struggle the nation pined for. These beaches, he told the crowd, were 'part of Australia', as if one small strip of Turkish coastline was somehow more sacred Australian territory than Australia itself. The soil that ran with the blood of the Anzacs was the true site of the nation's founding moment, a day of mourning held offshore, fifteen thousand kilometres away from the site of invasion, occupation and settlement. And this was not the only advantage. Over the previous decades, the ground-swell of new nationalism had been unable to invent a binding post-British myth of national identity. With Anzac's Imperial origins receding from public memory, the legend could now be refashioned as the Bastille Day or Fourth of July Australia never had, the day which cut Australia adrift from its Imperial past in one fell, heroic swoop, a story clearly yearned for, and much more romantic than the 'boring' history of incremental inde-pendence, epitomised by Bob Hawke's signing of the *Australia Act* in 1986. Six years before the Howard conservative govern-ment came to power, in March 1996, Anzac Day had already been re-packaged as the origin story of the green and gold. The ubiquitous photographs of the diggers – their roll-your-own cig-arettes hanging from the corner of their mouths, their slouch hats tilted back slightly to reveal the faces of chirpy, fey-like innocents – became the embodiment of Australian masculine character in adversity, whether on foreign football fields, the cricket pitches of England, fighting floods, or in the forests that raged with bushfires each summer.[12]

In the 1990s, newspaper and media coverage of Anzac Day increased significantly. Where coverage had previously con-sisted of a programme of events, an editorial, and a report of the march the following day, broadsheets now began to publish spe-cial 'Anzac lift-outs' in anticipation, some running up to eight pages in length. As the fiftieth anniversaries of the battles of World War 2 occurred with great regularity, the commemora-tion of war suddenly became an ongoing enterprise, with current affairs programmes producing finely choreographed odes to the veterans, showing images of the tear-lined faces of old soldiers which segued into shots of enthusiastic spectators waving Australian flags, all backed by the mandatory maudlin soundtrack.

Meanwhile, with unusual attention to the power of speech and ritual, Prime Minister Paul Keating wrote his own vision for Australia's future onto the Anzac legend, arguing that Australia's 'modern image' was formed not at Gallipoli but in the 1940s, in the jungles of Papua New Guinea and the waters of the South Pacific. These men and women had realised something new, Keating said, 'Australians had evolved into a different race'. Keating's insistence that the Anzacs had fought first for the empire, rather than for Australia, dovetailed perfectly with his republican agenda, just as his government's push for a more Asia-centred foreign policy fitted neatly with the story of Australian soldiers dying for the country in Asia fifty years earlier. Yet through his government's response to the *Mabo* decision (1992), and his Redfern Park speech (1993), he was also directly addressing the history of Indigenous dispossession in a way that no prime minister before him had attempted to do. In the wake of *Mabo*, the publication of the report into Aboriginal Deaths in Custody (1993), and the setting up of the Inquiry into The Stolen Generations, which was eventually published as *Bringing Them Home* in 1997, public debate was dominated by the post-colonial history of Aboriginal Australians, one that conservatives, led in 1996 by conservative prime minister, John Howard, recoiled from, painting it as overly negative and condemnatory of Australia's British heritage.[13]

On 25 April 1996, his first Anzac Day as prime minister, Howard signaled his response to the 'self-laceration' and 'guilt' of the Hawke-Keating era, announcing that he would enshrine the Australian flag in legislation, thereby ensuring that it could only be altered after a plebiscite or referendum. In the same breath, he wasted little time in identifying Anzac Day as the home of a new, more traditional and patriotic nationalism: 'It is particularly gratifying', he said, 'that some vestige of cynicism over Anzac Day a generation ago appears to have evaporated with young Australians taking more interest than ever before in Anzac Day and what it means for our national identity'. The *Australian*, as it would do for most of the next decade, responded enthusiastically. 'In the Anzacs can be found the model and inspiration for the nation's own self-esteem ... Anzac Day is Australia's genuine national day, transcending any other com- memoration.' Here was the nexus which would be made even more overt in the twenty-first century; national 'self-esteem' was not only illustrated through the story of Anzac, it would become dependent on it. To question or criticise the commemo- ration of Anzac Day would soon be the same as criticising the nation itself. As 25 April became the key pillar of national pride under Howard, Anzac Day ascended to the realm of sacred parable, a body of national myth that rested not on the history of the campaign, so much as it did on Australians' need for a 'national day' which was both a source of pride and one com- pletely free from feelings of guilt and shame.[14]

Between 1997 and 1999, the first years of John Howard's prime ministership, the national media carried hundreds of first-hand testaments from members of the Stolen Generations. Public demand for an official government apology by 2001 (the date designated for the formal completion of the process of rec- onciliation) became almost deafening. Howard resisted, arguing that there was no need to atone for policies which had been introduced by previous administrations. Unlike Anzac, the his- tory of past 'blemishes' on the national story, he argued, could not be linked to the present generation of Australians. Reconciliation was a practical matter, not symbolic: there would be no apology. Turning away from the 'Black armband' of Indigenous history and the symbolism of reconciliation, with its religious language of atonement, Howard embraced Anzac Day as a 'positive' counter-narrative, telling the Australians assembled at Anzac Cove for the Dawn Service on Anzac Day 2000, that the Anzacs had left them a national 'creed', a heritage of 'personal courage and initiative', which had given Australia a 'common purpose'. Standing on soil 'rich with the lives of our kin', Howard vowed to 'finish' what the Anzacs 'began'. As he told Channel Nine's *A Current Affair* shortly afterwards, there was a 'resurgence of national feeling, a passion for the Anzac legend and tradition amongst young Australians'.[15]

In the wake of 11 September 2001, and the *Tampa* election which followed in November 2001, Howard succeeded in harnessing a more defensive national mood, one which, in a time of war and global terrorism, was now even more in need of binding sites of national communion. In late 1999, Australian forces led the United Nations' International Force for East Timor. Only one month after 11 September, one thousand Australian troops joined the American and British forces in invading Afghanistan. The following year, in October 2002, the Bali bombings resulted in the death of two hundred and two people, including eighty-eight Australians. Six months later, in early 2003, Australian forces joined the American invasion of Iraq. Under attack from Islamic extremists, liberal democracies – the United States, Britain, Australia, and many countries in Western Europe – began to define the democratic values they sought to defend.

Within this broad international context John Howard elevated the Anzac legend. So much of the theatre and ritual of his prime ministership was performed on a military platform; he became the prime-ministerial impresario of countless welcome-home parades for returning Australian troops, the leader who spoke of an 'Australian military tradition', and the politician who sensed that in a volatile international climate, the Australian people were particularly receptive to the 'Anzac spirit' as the means through which they could express their common values and their dependence on one another. Schools were instructed to fly Australian flags, while 'Australian values' posters, which included a silhouette of Jack Simpson and his donkey, were also distributed. From the moment he was elected in 1996, until he was finally defeated by Kevin Rudd in 2007, Howard publicly encouraged the increasing numbers of Australians visiting Gallipoli each year. His Anzac Day speeches reflected the spirit of the times, yet at the same time, they attempted to cast the Anzac legend in the image of conservative nationalism, elevating 25 April to such an exalted position, that it became a completely new type of national day. Contrary to popular belief, this change was not a 'resurgence', rather, it was a revolution, a complete transformation of the traditional language and patterns of commemoration associated with the day.[16]

In attempting to mould the Anzac story, Howard offered the usual examples of rhetorical excess, claiming that Anzac Day occupied an 'eternal place in the Australian soul', and insisting that Gallipoli had shaped the character and the destiny of this country 'more than any other tradition or influence'. But the most significant change occurred after 2001, when he introduced a 'celebratory' tone into Anzac Day. He began to see Anzac Day as an occasion for 'the *celebration* of some wonderful values', and urged Australians to 'collectively *rejoice* in the growing embrace of that great tradition'. 'On this day', Howard proclaimed in 2003, 'we *enrich* ourselves', 'a nation reveals itself not only by the *men* it produces but by the *men* it honours, the *men* it remembers'. Broadsheet editorials chimed in, describing Anzac Day as a day which 'salutes the country itself', the day on which Australians 'celebrate' their 'founding generation'. Never before had Anzac Day been seen as a day of 'celebration'. Since the first Anzac ceremonies in 1916, words such as 'commemorate', 'remember' and 'mourn', together with phrases like 'pay our respects', reflected the tenor of the day. Far from a resurgence of 'the Anzac tradition', Howard was using Anzac Day as a vehicle for national self-congratulation. Australia Day was also infected, reflecting a growing culture of unreflective, patriotic display, best illustrated in Howard's Australia Day address in 2007, in which he declared without irony: 'We think we're pretty good and we are'.[17]

Some of the Anzac 'pilgrims', who were indulging in what Howard called 'a patriotic rite of passage' by visiting Anzac Cove, echoed the prevailing mood, providing the media with vox pops which suggested that the last thing on their minds was the history of World War 1: 'It wasn't about the Empire it was about us'; 'I am here because it's just great to be so proud of our history'; 'the diggers would be happy if they knew we were here'; 'they fought for us so that we could have a free life'; 'they're the reason why we live the way we do'. With Australian troops serving in several theatres overseas, Howard went to great lengths to place the fight against terrorism in 'the Anzac tradition'. The soldiers who 'died for our freedom' on the beaches of Anzac Cove in 1915, he argued, were the antecedents of the men who served in Iraq or Afghanistan. Australia's 'military tradition', said Howard, was continuous and 'peaceful'. We were not invaders. We were not killers. As he told an audience at Australia

House in London, late in 2003:

> Australians are not by nature a war like people. There is no
> tradition of conquest or imperial ambition. We've had no
> history of bloody civil war; of winning our independence
> through armed insurrection or fortifying our borders against
> some constant military threat ... and Gallipoli itself, the
> ultimate symbol of our military tradition, was not a glorious
> victory but a bloody stalemate and then a forced withdrawal
> ... Anzac Day remains more evocative of the Australian spirit
> than any other day in our calendar.[18]

Howard had found the narrative of 'national pride' he had
yearned for since his first years as Opposition leader in the
1980s, when he had distanced his party from the history of
shame promoted by the left in the lead up to the bicentenary.
Turning his back on the frontier warfare that accompanied the
history of settlement in Australia, he saw in Anzac, an 'uplift-
ing' history of 'honour'. Anzac allowed him to speak in mystical
language in a way no other aspect of Australia's past could do.
He described Australians on 25 April as being 'drawn together
almost by instinct, by a great silent summons to repay a debt to
the past ... [to] those they seek to honour'. The Anzac story was
entirely free from the 'blemishes' and 'stains' of Australia's colonial past, and it contained all the ingredients that neither the
foundation of a penal colony, nor the undramatic story of Federation could ever equal; a heroic history of sacrifice and action,
a history of service and duty, a history that could be cast in
the image of contemporary Australian liberalism – loyal, patriotic, and entirely free from the taint of rebellion – a glowing
'national inheritance' which could be cherished and revered.[19]

During Howard's last term (2004–07), one of the most

common features of the Anzac-led nationalism was a tendency to condemn the unpatriotic past of the 1960s and 1970s. Introducing *Today's* Anzac Day report in 2006, Tracey Grimshaw could barely contain herself: 'In the 1960s, many historians predicted that Anzac Day would go into decline as the diggers themselves died away. How wrong they were!' Presenting the ABC's *First Tuesday Book Club*, in 2007, and discussing the opposition to Anzac Day in the 1960s and 1970s, Jennifer Byrne remarked 'we're over all that now, aren't we?' In 2005, conservative commentator, Gerard Henderson, suggested that the time had come to stop singing Eric Bogle's folk ballad 'And the Band Played Waltzing Matilda'. Quoting the last line from the penultimate verse of Bogle's song: 'And the young people ask "What are they marching for?" and I ask meself the same question', Henderson accused Bogle of failing 'to anticipate the revival of interest by Australians in their history'. 'The ninetieth anniversary of Anzac Day', he argued, 'would be an appropriate time to despatch Eric Bogle's message to the musical graveyard'. Between 1996 and 2007, conservative politicians frequently cast their own patriotic virtue against the image of a radical, disloyal past. Howard, for example, often bemoaned the failure of Australians in the 1960s and 1970s to 'welcome home' those who had fought in Vietnam, just as he regretted that generation's criticism of Anzac Day. By 2007, Howard's view had shaped the dominant popular memory of the 1960s and 1970s. By representing Anzac Day as under attack by radicals of earlier decades, Howard could more easily assume the mantle of its saviour.[20]

As chapter three shows there was certainly much opposition to Anzac Day, which began in the late 1950s, with attacks in student newspapers well before the movement against the war gained momentum in the late 1960s. There was also the expectation that the ritual of Anzac Day might well die with the diggers, as the final words of Eric Bogle's anthem assumed: '... year after year those old men disappear, soon no one will march there at all'. In London, on Anzac Day 1968, protesters at the Cenotaph in Whitehall laid their own wreath: 'Vietnam explodes Anzac myth'. They also carried banners demonstrating their support for the Vietcong. 'Angry Anzac veterans ripped down and trampled the banners, and fights broke out'. The following year in Perth, student protesters attempted unsuccessfully to lay a wreath remembering 'the murdered Vietnamese', before scuffles broke out with police. In 1966, when a Sydney woman ran from the crowd during a welcome home parade for soldiers returning from Vietnam, and tried to smear marching soldiers with red paint, her action was shown live on ABC TV, and the image gradually came to be seen as the embodiment of opposition to the Vietnam War. Yet until the last years of the war, the overwhelming response of Australians was largely supportive. Vietnam veterans were officially welcomed home and they were not poorly treated. However, they had been militarily defeated fighting a war that aroused considerable opposition. Their sense of exile and exploitation fuelled their sense of grievance, which would later play a powerful role in securing their recognition as Anzacs. While numbers watching Anzac Day parades in the 1960s and 1970s fluctuated wildly, never did the number of spectators reach such a critically low point that the day was in danger of disappearing altogether. In 1965, on the fiftieth anniversary of Anzac Day, the *Sydney Morning Herald* captured the anxiety and uncertainty in the country's commemoration of the Anzacs.

Many Australians are no longer willing to regard the day as a national day, but see it simply as a commemoration of a bloody – and unsuccessful – campaign on a remote peninsula ... certainly the day is no longer taken for granted as it was in the years between the war ... [yet] the numbers of the marchers all over the country and, more importantly, the size of the crowds which watched them, surely showed that the day has not lost its grip on the hearts and minds of Australians ... its form may change in time, but it will not die.[21]

Two years later, Rupert Murdoch's newspaper, the *Australian*, which began publication in 1964, condemned the 'crippling artificiality' of Australia Day, but insisted that Anzac Day had survived 'the boredom of an older generation' and even 'the scepticism of a younger', to bind Australians 'in a mysterious even unwilling communion with one another'. 'Anzac Day', argued the *Australian*, 'expresses, as no other day or symbol can, something that we understand and nobody else can'.

Despite the criticism of Anzac Day at this time, the press remained firmly behind the retention of 25 April as Australia's only national day, largely for three reasons. The political class, together with most opinion makers, knew, as the *Australian* suggested on 25 April 1969, that the Australian people had yet to reach 'definitive agreement' on the form their new national identity would take. With Australia Day little more than an excuse for a holiday, it was unthinkable to allow the grasp of 25 April on the nation's imagination to slip. Australians were wrestling not only with anti-war protest movement in the 1970s, but also with the challenge of reinventing Anzac Day, trying to change it from an Imperial ritual, to a crucible of purely Australian national identity. It was for this reason, during Anzac Day ceremonies in the early 1970s, that there was such fierce resistance to 'Advance Australia Fair' being played as the national anthem instead of 'God Save the Queen'. As the *Australian* recognised, it was crucial to show that Anzac Day, and the rising wave of 'new nationalism', presented 'no contradiction'. Moreover, in the absence of widespread monarchical allegiance, only Anzac Day contained the necessary elements of mystery and spirituality that could truly bind the Australian people. Finally, at a time when Australia's foreign policy priorities in the wake of Britain's entry into the European Economic Community were undergoing rapid transformation, many commentators were acutely aware of the potential political utility of Anzac Day. In 1965, the *West Australian* saw the purpose of Anzac Day as helping Australia to face 'the perils' of the years to come, 'whether it comes militarily from Peking or Djakarta, [or] diplomatically from the new and fumbling forces at work in Asia and Africa'. In 1967, as national servicemen and regular army volunteers marched together on Anzac Day for the first time 'as veterans of Vietnam', the *Sydney Morning Herald* saw the advantage of retaining Anzac Day as a focal point of national unity.

> We face, with the contraction of British power, the prospect
> of very much heavier regional defence responsibilities.
> Whether or not Britain, after joining the European Common
> Market, decides to pull out of Asia altogether (except for
> a token force in Hong Kong, and perhaps a few bombers
> in Australia) it is now abundantly clear that the scale
> of her troop withdrawals will be much greater than was
> indicated earlier. This does not mean that Australia will
> have physically to take over Britain's role; but it does mean

that we will be much more exposed and will have to make a greater defence effort.[22]

Australians were suddenly confronted with a new framework of national and international politics, and they struggled to adapt the language of their traditional mythologies to a profoundly different set of challenges. In the Anzac Day 'resurgence' of recent years, much of this past has been misremembered. Just as we have grown accustomed to using Anzac Day as a means of inflating national pride, so we have grown more adept at forgetting our history. While the history of Aboriginal dispossession and cultural annihilation is wheeled out for ceremonial apology before we 'move on', the Anzac legend is held in a state of perpetual remembrance. We have forgotten earlier stories of national self-definition and national values and the struggles waged by those who have come before us to build a distinctive, democratic and egalitarian society. And we have forgotten the divisions caused by our participation in overseas battles and more generally the terrible costs of war. We have misremembered the past in order to bury a history of debate, both around Anzac Day and the politics of war, fearful perhaps, at a time of global uncertainty, that similar divisions might erupt and disturb the ranks of our present-day patriotic army.

As our political leaders increasingly mimic the public performances of American politicians, smiling and waving to the cameras as they pass through the church gates on Sunday morning, one wonders if the Anzac revolution has occurred not because we are a post-Christian society, but because we live in a time of religious revival. Before Anzac, we bow down, we close ranks and we remain silent. So sacrosanct has Anzac Day become, that no political leader dare risk qualifying, let alone doubting, the absolute centrality of its position to our national identity and national values.

In our rush to participate in the Anzac 'resurgence' as the centenary of the Gallipoli invasion approaches in 2015, we appear to have forgotten to ask the most fundamental question of all. After the horrors of war in the twentieth century, in which so many millions of people died, does Australia, a modern pluralist democracy in the twenty-first century, still wish to cling to a nineteenth century concept of nationhood: the belief that a nation can only be truly borne through the spilling of the sacrificial blood of its young?

—6—

How do schoolchildren learn about the spirit of Anzac?

Marilyn Lake

'Anzac history certainly generates more education
funding than any other areas of Australia's past.'

Anna Clark, *History's Children: History Wars in the Classroom*,
UNSW Press, Sydney, 2008, p 49

During the last ten years a veritable tidal wave of military history has engulfed our nation, generating the torrent of curriculum materials sent to primary and secondary schools by the Department of Veterans' Affairs (DVA),[1] the endless stories and supplements in newspapers and other media, new documentary television series, live broadcasts of the Dawn Service from Gallipoli, travelling national and local museum exhibits, the Anzac Lecture Series and exhibitions at the Shrine of Remembrance in Melbourne, the expansion of memorials across the country and the publication of an unprecedented number of books in the field of war history, often made possible by subsidies from the DVA, the Australian Army History Unit of the Department of Defence, the Returned Services League (RSL) and the Australian War Memorial, which also has an affiliated Facebook site, encouraging members to 'become a fan' of the Anzacs. Joint ventures are common, for example, Michael Caulfield's book, *Voices of War: Stories from the Australians at War Film Archive*, based on the documentary series commissioned by the DVA and the ABC's *Gallipoli: The First Day.*[2]

According to a recent estimate, books published on Australia at war increased from less than sixty in the 1970s to over two hundred and fifty in the 1980s, to more than three hundred and sixty in the 1990s, a number likely to be soon exceeded in this decade. No aspect of war history has been ignored. Personal testimony jostles alongside studies of military strategy, individual stories compete with major battles. Titles during the last five years include: Frank Glen *Bowler of Gallipoli: Witness to the Anzac Legend*, Richard Reid *Gallipoli 1915*, Kevin Meade *Heroes before Gallipoli: Bita Paka and That One Day in September*, Stephen Chambers *Anzac: The Landing*, Peter Hart *Gallipoli: A Stone Unturned*, Victor Rudenno *Gallipoli: Attack from the Sea*, Chris Clark *Naval Aviation at Gallipoli*, Peter Pedersen *The Anzacs: Gallipoli to the Western Front*, Jane Pearson *Anzacs at Gallipoli: Creating a Legend*, Alistair Thomson *Anzac Stories: Using Personal Testimony in War*, Jonathan King *The Western Front Diaries: The ANZACS' Own Story Battle by Battle*, Wesley Olson *Gallipoli: The Western Australian Story*, Bruce Scates *Return to Gallipoli: Walking the Battlefields of the Great War*, Les Carlyon's *The Great War*, EPF Lynch *Somme Mud: The War Experiences of an Australian Infantryman in France 1916–1919*, Peter Cochrane *Tobruk 1941*, Michael Tyquin *Madness and the Military: Australia's Experience of the Great War*, Melanie Oppenheimer *Oceans of Love: Narrelle – An Australian Nurse in World War 1*, Bart

Ziino *A Distant Grief*, Peter Stanley *Quinn's Post: Anzac, Gallipoli* and *Men of Mont St Quentin* and Elena Govor *Russian Anzacs in Australian History*. In this ever-growing industry, war commemoration and writing history have become conflated, joined in a grand narrative about the seminal role of Australian military engagements and the Anzac spirit in shaping the nation.

This chapter focusses on the role of the DVA in militarising our history in schools during the last ten years. In his *Quadrant* address in 2006, former prime minister, John Howard, talked of the need for Australian children to be 'taught their national inheritance'.[3] That heritage in all its richness and diversity, and not just one aspect of it, should indeed be available to all Australians. Schoolchildren are now conceptualised as the inheritors of the Anzac spirit and its custodians. They have been bombarded in recent years and throughout the year with every aspect of the history of our engagement in overseas wars. Indeed lessons begin even before children begin school. One correspondent wrote to me: 'My son whilst a four-year-old last year received an extensive age appropriate grounding in ANZAC traditions at his pre-school!' We might well doubt the former prime minister's assertion that 'we have never had a warlike tradition we Australians'. Schoolchildren would be forgiven for thinking that this is our dominant national tradition. And it seems that many do think this. Anna Clark in her survey of schoolchildren's attitudes to Australian history was surprised at how many students now assume that a 'militarised national identity' is 'intrinsically Australian'. She was also concerned that these lessons were generating nationalist sentiment rather than 'historical understanding'.[4]

The vast pedagogical enterprise of the DVA – which under its Commemorative Activities programme has supplied all schools in Australia, primary and secondary, with voluminous and sophisticated curriculum materials, websites, virtual tours of the battlefields, handsome prizes including trips to Gallipoli and other battlefields – has been made possible by massive funding from the federal government, the budget for this activity increasing from \$4 215 000 in 2001–02 to \$5 878 000 in 2007–08. Whether it is the job of the federal Department of Veterans' Affairs to prescribe schoolchildren's understanding of national history is surely debatable. Whether it should link these history lessons to the definition and promotion of national values is more questionable still. Has the equivalent happened in any other democratic country?

History has been appropriated in Australia for militarist purposes and comprehensively re-written in the process. The myth of Anzac has been at the heart of the reshaping of public memory through a national story that defines military values as Australian values and overseas battlefields as key historic sites. The relentless militarisation of Australian history has effectively marginalised other stories, different historic sites and other conceptions of national values. Writing history is not a choice between narrative and a stew of themes, as former prime minister, John Howard, liked to declare, or between fact and interpretation as our current prime minister suggests, but it does involve a choice between narratives. Which narratives about our past gain ascendancy depends on their proponents' material and discursive resources as well as on their rhetorical power and dramatic appeal. As historians we think it's important to distinguish between history and mythology.

Significance of war to our national development

From the late 1990s, the federal government through its agencies, the DVA and the Australian War Memorial replaced the RSL – aged and out of touch – as the new promoters of Anzac, deploying their vast resources to promulgate a new national history, a story of national development centred on the sacrifice and service of the Anzacs through the ages. Providing extensive curriculum materials, teaching resources and websites to schools, through its own publications and publication subsidies, the funding of documentary films and travelling museum exhibits as well as the expansion and renovation of community war memorials, the federal government has lent its authority and vast resources to a new pedagogical project we might call the militarisation of Australian history.

The History Wars of the 1990s provided a key context and motivation for the focus on twentieth century wartime history, with former prime minister John Howard especially keen to divert attention from the history of Aboriginal dispossession and frontier massacres by opening up a new front. A celebratory national narrative was needed to defeat the critical force of 'Black armband history' and to replace the earlier radical nationalist tradition, disliked by the right and discredited on the left by feminist and anti-racist critiques from the 1970s through the 1980s. There was clearly little to be gained from endlessly disputing the extent of frontier massacres as Keith Windschuttle had done.[5] Far easier to change the subject and offer an alternative story of the forging of national identity in overseas wars: the Boer War, World Wars 1 and 2, the Malayan Emergency, Korea, Vietnam, the Gulf War, Iraq and Afghanistan.

At the centre of the new national narrative promoted by

the DVA was the sacrifice and service of Australian soldiers and their role in shaping the nation. Attacking the RSL, as the protagonists in the anti-war play *The One Day of the Year* had done was one thing. Appearing to attack the Anzacs was quite another. The RSL was a special interest group lobbying for its constituency. As national heroes, the Anzacs could be seen to be above politics. A significant and symbolic change in terminology occurred: that very Australian group 'returned servicemen' suddenly became 'veterans', as those who served in Vietnam and then the government itself borrowed the American terminology.

The effect of the educational campaigns of the last decade – documented below – has been to disarm the critique of Australian participation in war by casting it as an attack on Anzac and the nation itself. It has also worked to marginalise other accounts of the formation of national values, civic, social and political traditions and different Australians' experiences.

In 1994 the federal government led by Labor prime minister, Paul Keating, first became involved in actively funding community activities to commemorate Australian engagement in war. On the fiftieth anniversary of the end of World War 2 he announced the 'Australia Remembers' programme, presided over by veterans' affairs minister Con Sciacca, whose personal commitment did much to ensure its great success. Introduced as the largest series of commemorations ever held in Australian history, it also promised 'job opportunities' for seven hundred unemployed Australians.[6] 'Australia Remembers' was hailed as a new nation-building programme embracing local communities across Australia.

There was then no general commemorations programme within the DVA beyond the Office of Australian War Graves, which managed a war graves programme, established during World War 1 to assure bereaved families that relatives killed on active service, whose bodies would not be returned, were properly buried and commemorated. The objective of the war graves programme, whose responsibilities dated back to 1917, was thus defined as:

> To commemorate, individually, the sacrifice of those
> Australian men and women who gave their lives during, or as
> a result of, their service to Australia and the Commonwealth
> in war, or who were prisoners of war, and to maintain these
> commemorations.[7]

The war graves programme was focussed on appropriate burial practices, with names inscribed at gravesites or on memorials, in lawn cemeteries, crematoria or gardens of remembrance. A research service was also provided for next of kin and others seeking information about burial sites and it supplied photographs of individual graves, war cemeteries and memorials for those unable to travel overseas.

The 'Australia Remembers' programme in 1995 inaugurated a new direction in commemoration: it emphasised historical education. Allan Hawke, president of the Repatriation Commission, noted in his report that:

> Activities associated with the commemorative year brought
> to the attention of younger Australians a reminder of the
> sacrifice and commitment shown by their forebears in
> the dark days of more than fifty years ago and a greater
> understanding of the Commission's ongoing and vital role
> in compensating veterans, their widows, widowers and
> dependants for the effects of service.

The repatriation work of the commission – dealing with the long-term damaging effects of service – was traditionally central to the Repatriation Commission's brief. In 1996, its four programmes were defined as Compensation, Health Care and Services, War Graves and Corporate Services. History lessons had not yet assumed a major role in the work of the department, but this would soon change.

Following the public impact of the 'Australia Remembers' programme, the new president of the commission, Neil Johnston together with Minister Bruce Scott announced in 1996 a new commemorative programme defined as 'Their Service – Our Heritage' to prepare for the centenary of Federation. It was

> aimed at recognising the contribution of veterans to the building of this nation as we approach the centenary celebration of Australian Federation and will ensure that the sacrifices of the veteran community continue to be remembered.

Beginning in 1997, 'Their Service – Our Heritage' incorporated five key elements: national days of remembrance, memorials, significant events, education and community awareness. Its educational aim was clear: 'to educate all Australians, through school-based and other programmes, about the service and sacrifice of Australia's veterans and their role in developing the nation'.

In 1996–97 grants dispersed by the Local Commemorative Activities Fund exceeded one million dollars and were mainly used to repair or construct over eight hundred community-based war memorials. Community awareness campaigns were also initiated to encourage the preservation of memorials, medals and memorabilia. Two booklets, *Memories and Memorabilia* and

Valuing our Veterans explained the importance of preserving wartime heritage and the recorded memories of returned service men and women, with school students encouraged to record veterans' experiences, including, of course, the memories of their own relatives.

The identification of wartime heritage was an ever-expanding project. In the president's overview of the activities of the Repatriation Commission and the DVA for 1999–2000, he noted that although the forthcoming centenary of Federation marked one hundred years of nationhood, Australian involvement in overseas wars and conflicts preceded Federation.

> October 1999 marked the centenary of the beginning of the Boer War and the year was notable for major commemorative activities to honour a century of service by Australians. There were strong attendances at the dedication of the Australian Services Nurses National Memorial and the Australian National Korean War Memorial in Canberra ... Their Service – Our Heritage has played an important role in promoting the community's interest in commemoration and this was recognised in the 2001–02 budget, when the Program was extended for four years.

The 'Sharing their Legacy' project was funded under this programme in a $60 000 partnership with the History Trust of South Australia, which by 2001 supported seventeen projects and exhibitions on wartime history. It brought together veterans, schoolchildren, historical societies and museums in rural and metropolitan South Australia. This was extended with a further grant to the History Trust of $10 150 to provide 'An Enduring Legacy' in the form of a conference, website and special edition of the journal *Community History*. The DVA also provided $250 000 to the Australian War Memorial to stage a travelling exhibitions programme.

The education programme was developed in conjunction with state departments of education, history teachers' associations, *Studies [of Society and Environment]* magazine, which featured regular articles on Gallipoli, Anzac Day and other events in the military history calendar. The DVA also worked with the Australian War Memorial, which supported the National History Challenge, the schools competition with its special category of wartime history, providing a competition for students in years 5 to 12.

In preparation for Anzac Day in the year 2000, the DVA distributed Anzac Day school kits to all primary and secondary schools across Australia. Because Anzac Day coincided with school holidays that year, the DVA also sent kits to Scouts and Guides associations, the YMCA and the YWCA, 'to encourage them to involve young people in activities to help them better understand the Anzac tradition'. The kit included activity sheets, classroom exercises based on the book *Anzacs, The Pain and the Glory of Gallipoli* by Peter Bowers and published by Australia Post.[8]

Other material included posters, information about the Australian War Memorial's 'Memorial Boxes' and the Simpson Prize, an essay-based competition for year 9 students, focussing on the Gallipoli legend. The eight Simpson Prize winners visited the Australian War Memorial in February and in April travelled to Gallipoli to attend the dedication of the ANZAC commemorative site. The DVA annual report for 1999–2000 was pleased with the outcome: the Simpson Prize was regarded as a great success in 'encouraging young Australians to find out more about the Anzac legend and its place in our history'.[9]

Some parents became concerned about these developments, but felt unable to query this emphasis in their children's education. One mother told me that her son 'did military history last year in school and was asked to submit an essay for the Simpson Prize'. The winner was offered a trip to Gallipoli to see where Australian history really happened. Her son found it all pretty 'gagging'.

In the new millennium, military history continued to expand. With preparations for the centenary of Federation in 2001 in full swing, the DVA provided $100 000 for a specific wartime heritage component in 'The People's Voice', a National Council for the Centenary of Federation community history website project. More generally the DVA conceptualised its contribution as the preservation of military heritage and the defining of a wartime legacy:

> Through the Department of Veterans' Affairs, Australia honours its commitment to acknowledge and commemorate the service and sacrifice of Australians in wars, defence and peacekeeping services. The Department works to ensure that the legacy of Australia's wartime heritage is preserved and passed on to new generations.[10]

A key initiative was the production of the ambitious eight-part television documentary series *Australians at War*, a joint venture between the DVA and the Australian War Memorial, for which five million dollars had been provided in the 1999 federal budget. Its aims were to:

- mark the centenary of Federation by documenting Australia's involvement in major wars and conflicts during the past 100 years;

- explore how the Australian experience of war has helped shape the nation;
- communicate this heritage to all Australians, especially young people; and
- provide a continuing resource for educational and community purposes.

To this end the production company established its own website and research service.

In the same year, the federal budget provided $4.4 million to complete Nominal Rolls commemorating those who have served in Australia's defence forces since Federation. The World War 2 Nominal Roll required the data conversion of some 1.3 million service records, to be placed on the departmental website to be linked to the Boer War and World War 1 databases developed by the Australian War Memorial and National Archives. These would provide crucial information not only to researchers, but to families wishing to identify their relatives' war service records. The federal government was pleased with what had been achieved and in the 2000 federal budget allocated another $17.2 million to extend 'Their Service – Our Heritage' for another four years beyond the centenary of Federation.

The national commitment to the expansion of war commemoration and military history seemed unstoppable. New opportunities were identified in the revitalisation of Remembrance Day on 11 November, the anniversary of the armistice that ended World War 1. Governor-General Sir William Deane urged all Australians to take seriously the obligation to observe one minute's silence at eleven am. The DVA created the Remembrance Day 'Education Resource: We Remember' targeted at lower primary students and their teachers, with a 'big book' *Remembrance Day*, teachers' guides and student activities. It was believed to be the first such resource designed for the younger age group.

'Targeting educational initiatives for young people'

Commemorative activities were designed to reach right across the nation, into all corners of the community, but the main focus was history education in primary and secondary schools. With the inauguration of the new programme, 'Saluting their Service', in 2002, the focus on schools intensified with a team of 'education service providers' established to provide quality curriculum resources. The DVA also extended sponsorship to state and national history teachers' associations, their annual conferences and journals. As the annual report stated the department wanted to ensure that the 'community better appreciates the significance of wartime experiences to our development as a nation'. The pedagogical note was becoming more strident.

From 1997 the commemoration of national days of remembrance – Anzac Day, Remembrance Day, VP Day – had been a key strategy in the shaping of public memory. With Australians engaged in war for much of the twentieth century every year provided new possibilities for anniversary events. In 2002, the DVA gave presentations and staged displays at the national conference of the History Teachers' Association of Australia in Sydney to 'broaden teachers' awareness' of the sixtieth anniversaries of 1942 wartime events. Teachers needed educating as well as students. The December issue of the New South Wales journal, *Teaching History* focussed accordingly on 'Australia at war'.

Since 2002, all eleven thousand two hundred schools in Australia have been the recipients of curriculum materials that can be used not just on special anniversaries, such as Anzac Day, Remembrance Day, VP Day or Vietnam Veterans' Day, but as part of the everyday curriculum. The DVA annual report 2002–03 included a special section candidly named: 'Targeting educational initiatives for young people'. It was a busy year. Schoolchildren took lessons directing them to 'learn about and acknowledge the events of our wartime years [and] the significance of those events in shaping our nation'. As well as take history lessons in the classroom, students were 'encouraged to participate in commemorative events in their communities'. State-of-the-art enquiry-based methodologies were encouraged, equipping students for life-long learning.

Educational resources were now specifically crafted by 'professional educators' specially employed to meet the needs of different state curricula and subject designs, including 'studies in society and the environment' and 'history', and specially designed for different levels of learning appropriate to secondary and primary school students. In 2002, the DVA distributed the 'Australians at War' education resources, which complemented the *Australians at War* documentary TV series and website, and included a specially produced compilation video and teachers' guide. The three video set of the documentary series was sent to all secondary schools in Australia.

Then there was 'Time To Remember: Understanding Australia's Experiences in War and Peacekeeping', 'an education resource for lower to middle primary school students' distributed to all Australian primary schools in April 2003. 'Time To Remember' included sixteen big picture cards, a teachers' guide and Anzac Day information pack. The pack was also sent to all secondary schools. Another resource for primary students was *We Remember*: a full colour illustrated big book for lower primary students and teachers. 'The aim of the book is to educate young Australians about the contributions made by Australian servicemen and women in shaping the nation and its traditions.' Other resources included 'Our Past – Our Future: Commemorating Remembrance Day', 'Working the Web: Investigating Australia's Wartime History' and 'Australia's Wartime History: A Guide to Commemorations Resources' and specially for primary schools, an entire Primary School Work Unit 'The Australian Experience: Anzac Spirit' which was defined as 'the core values which epitomise Australians in war including endurance, courage, ingenuity, good humour and mateship'.

Other ways of engaging school students included competitions such as the National History Challenge, the Simpson Prize and the Anzac Day Schools' Activities Awards, the latter administered by the History Teachers' Association of Victoria to encourage the now possibly wearying students to find 'new and creative ways of commemorating Anzac Day' while continuing 'to observe tradition and include veterans in their activities'. In 2002, a total of one hundred and seventeen entries were received, many using video and computer technology in their presentations. The DVA reported: 'All reflected a high degree of enthusiasm in their schools for commemorating Anzac Day and the awards represent an important feedback mechanism for monitoring interest in these commemorative events in schools.'[11]

DVA educators recognised the importance of engaging young people through the use of 'innovative technologies':

The importance of recording veterans' experiences in
a structured, accessible format was recognised and the

Australians at War Film Archive initiated. Innovative
technology is being used to present Australia's wartime
history though multimedia and in a way that it is more
accessible and understandable to the wider community,
particularly younger Australians. The *Visit Gallipoli* and
Australians at War websites continued to be developed
and work commenced on a new website about Australia's
involvement in World War 11.[12]

There was a new focus on pedagogical concerns and the importance of identifying the needs of teachers. 'The Department has
worked closely with educators', advised the 2002–03 annual
report 'to focus on resource materials that meet the needs of
teachers and students'. Professional history educators were
employed to produce state-of-the-art materials that would make
school teachers' preparation of lessons so much easier.[13]

DVA's educational work with schools was supplemented by
a local grants scheme whereby community organisations were
offered payments of $4000 each should they wish to promote
the department's priorities: the restoration of memorials, the
construction of new memorials, the writing of unit histories
and organisation of reunions, the commemoration of military
anniversaries, the support of research programmes in schools
and building links with local museums to preserve and display
wartime heritage.

Websites were continually developed, enhanced and
updated. The DVA annual report for 2003–04 was pleased to
record a remarkable 'measure of success' and suggested that its
commemorative work was reaching more people than its other
activities related to the provision of veteran services:

The commemorations components of the DVA website and the websites commissioned by the Department to tell the stories of Australians' war experiences since the Anglo-Boer war, at Gallipoli and during World War 2 have attracted significant visitor numbers and have added substantially to accessible, informative data on our wartime history ... Visitor numbers to the commemorations pages on the DVA website greatly increased. There were 275 134 visitors to the commemorations pages during 2003–04. This was an increase of more than 53 000 visitors compared to the previous year. Commemorations pages also featured as four out of the top five DVA pages visited for that month.

There was a further increase of forty-five per cent in visitors to the commemorations pages on the DVA website between 2004 and 2005.

But this was by no means the full extent of their 'promotional activities'. Education materials were also sent out in hard copy and in the form of compact discs and posters, to those who mightn't have the time or resources to access the internet, as well as to politicians for use in their 'electoral work':

Community awareness of and participation in commemorative activities continued to be promoted through a range of initiatives such as the distribution of Anzac Day and Remembrance Day posters and compact discs for the conduct of commemorative ceremonies to schools, aged care facilities, ex-service organisations and Federal Members and Senators.[14]

Through 'Saluting their Service', the DVA provided further funding – another $750 000 in 2004–05 – to the Australian

War Memorial's travelling exhibition programme. Twenty-five new exhibitions were developed and displayed at three hundred and ten locations around the country.

Funding was also provided for major exhibitions in Canberra at the Australian War Memorial ('The Dawn of the Legend' $86500) and Old Parliament House ('My Melancholy Duty' $125000). Regional initiatives including a South Australian exhibition on Gallipoli and a play sponsored by the Queensland Arts Council about Australian nurses interned in Malaya were together provided with $70000.

The year 2005 was heralded as a big one for war commemoration with both the ninetieth anniversary of the landing at Gallipoli and the sixtieth anniversary of the end of World War 2 attracting special rounds of funding. The 2004–05 budget provided another $15.1 million dollars to fund the commemorations programme over the following four years and this was supplemented by a further series of 'electorate grants' to enable community and ex-service groups to organise activities in each federal electorate to commemorate the sixtieth anniversary of the end of World War 2. During the same year the Australian War Memorial spent $3254000 on research, information and dissemination. Staff were pleased to report that they were in increasing demand as advisers and consultants to governments, other institutions, media and educational organisations.

Commemorative missions abroad departed for numerous destinations. The leaders of ten ex-service organisations were invited to represent 'the Australian veteran community' at the Gallipoli Anzac Day services. A commemorative mission party of seventeen veterans and one war widow together with the national presidents of the RSL and the Australian Veterans and Defence Services Council travelled to France and London in

May while another mission travelled to Borneo via Singapore.

Schoolchildren and teachers were supplied with even more resources. The DVA commissioned the Office of the Board of Studies in New South Wales to develop a resource to aid investigation of Australia's wartime history using DVA's websites 'Visit Gallipoli' and 'Australia's War 1939–1945'. The result was 'Operation CLICK: Anzac to Kokoda' which was distributed to all schools in March 2005.[15]

Guidelines encouraged community groups at home to involve schoolchildren and young people in activities that reinforced 'the notion of the debt we all owe for our freedom and democracy'. 'Indebtedness and gratitude', 'freedom and democracy': these became key general themes and schoolchildren learnt their lessons well. As Anna Clark found in her interviews with schoolchildren across Australia many now believe they owe everything to the Anzacs – 'If they weren't fighting Gallipoli, we wouldn't be where we are today'.[16]

To further recompense those who served in war and to commemorate the sixtieth anniversary of the end of World War 2, the Australian government asked the Royal Australian Mint to issue medallions to all surviving Australian veterans, widows and widowers from World War 2, as well as British Commonwealth and Allied veterans with qualifying service and the widows and widowers of those with qualifying service, now resident in Australia. It was estimated that some three hundred and twenty-five thousand medallions were required, but many of the recipients thought the money could surely have been better spent.

What is remarkable about all this activity is not that the DVA believes in the centrality of war to Australian history, but that it is funded so lavishly to make this case to schoolchildren and the larger community and that a federal department, established to take care of the needs of veterans and tend their graves, plays such a large role in the teaching of history in primary and secondary schools. Recently steps have been taken by the Department of Education, Employment and Workplace Relations to develop a National Curriculum including history as one of its four focus areas. It will be interesting to see how history as a critical practice, committed not to the inculcation of national pride, but to stimulate historical understanding of Australia's past and its place in the world, relates to DVA's promulgation of the Anzac tradition.

Debating war and history

The online debate in the *Age* last April about the meaning of Anzac and its place in our national history clearly reflected the lessons instilled by the educators from the DVA. The idea that Australian soldiers were always fighting for our 'freedom and democracy', that Anzac values were central to our national identity and that the 'spirit of Anzac' animated all past achievements – whether we were fighting wars or bushfires – were faithfully echoed in the online discussion. But there was also considerable disquiet about the sentimentalising of war and the nationalist uses now made of military service. There was concern that national memory was being warped into a propaganda tool to ensure support for the next war. 'Honouring/respecting ALL victims of war is important', wrote Ron. 'Revering them and elevating them to the status of hero is not. It may even be downright dangerous.'

The educators at the DVA have found partners in universities as well as museums and schools. Some universities have taken to the enterprise with enthusiasm. At Monash University the National Centre for Australian Studies is a partner in the 'Spirit of Anzac' competition prize study tour. Monash also offers a Monash–Gallipoli Prize, its historians have written a history of the Shrine of Remembrance and introduced two new units for undergraduate study, 'The ANZAC Battlefield Tour' and 'Anzac Legends: Australians at War'. In addition a community engagement programme conducts 'national conversations', the first of which was focussed on 'Sacred Places: War Memorials in the Australian Landscape' and offers an 'Outback Orations' programme, whose subject in 2008 was 'Broken Hill's Memory of the Great War'.

Many history teachers are now employed either directly by the DVA in designing state-of-the-art curriculum materials or as researchers, consultants, conference organisers and assessors on war related projects. Some have objected to our criticism of the militarisation of history by arguing that the curriculum materials are ever more inclusive with new units focussed on women at war, Aboriginal participation in overseas service (despite the tradition of discrimination against them) and debates about conscription. But their objections miss the point. Why is one federal government department funded to produce history materials when other federal government departments are not? Why not the departments of employment, health, immigration, environment and Aboriginal affairs? Might not they also be funded to educate schoolchildren and Australians more generally about the history of their activities and past achievements?

Many school teachers are concerned at the way in which the militarisation of Australian history has come to dominate the curriculum and are acutely aware of their dependence on the extensive resources now supplied by the DVA. They also report that students become emotionally engaged with the story of young men giving their lives at Gallipoli and on other battlefields, though as suggested in chapter one they rarely seem to discuss the fact of killing and the Anzacs' apparent skill and enthusiasm with the bayonet. 'Australian identity comes out of war' schoolchildren affirm. Learning about Australians at war, said a Canberra schoolgirl 'makes us appreciate, like, the Anzac spirit and everything that we celebrate about it and our nation because it was our birth as a nation as people say'. 'Most people say that you shape the country with the way you fight your battles and what comes from that', remarked an Adelaide schoolboy, who added that 'maybe it's just boys and guns'.[17]

In their identification with the story of Anzac, schoolchildren have been imbued with a new sense of patriotic pride, but in sentimentalising history and in celebrating military virtues we fear that history as a critical practice, and as a way of explaining and understanding the past, is in danger of succumbing to nationalist mythology. We are concerned furthermore that Australians' pioneering achievements in building a democratic society and a welfare state, in extending equal rights to women and to Indigenous Australians, in fostering multiculturalism and racial equality have been silenced by the resurgence of the dangerous nineteenth century idea that nations are made in war. We think it is time to reclaim our national values and commemorate the role of the Australians involved in campaigns for civil, social and political freedoms and who enshrined them in our national culture.

Moving on?

Henry Reynolds and Marilyn Lake

'Each year we wrestle with words to describe the
Anzac spirit. I don't think we ever do it the justice
it deserves, but we share a sense of it, and we've held
on to it since it emerged in World War One.'

Governor-General Quentin Bryce, *Australian*,
2 September 2009

Few members of the governor-general's audience or readers of
later published reports would have found anything unusual in
Her Excellency's recent remarks about Australian history. Her
explicit assumption that Australian identity and national character can be conflated with the Anzac spirit would have surprised no one. Such sentiments are commonplace, cherished and
comforting, and for that reason rarely questioned or subjected to
serious analysis. While, as a nation, we may wrestle with words
to describe it, we show far less interest in grappling with the
question of why we are obsessed with the Anzac spirit and now
accord it priority over almost every other aspect of our history.

The substance of this book should remind us that the close,
contemporary focus on Anzac has not been a constant feature
of Australian historical thinking. There has been opposition to

the militarism inherent in Anzac Day celebrations at various times since the 1920s and it intensified from the late 1950s. Many of the general histories written during the middle decades of the twentieth century paid little attention to it even though many of those historians had served in World War 2. At that time war history was seen as a specialist sub-discipline with little relevance to the mainstream of history. Australian history focussed on what had happened in Australia, not on what our soldiers had done overseas. The emphasis of Australian history was, as we have shown, on political and social reform and the shaping of a vision of a new society.

What we find remarkable, then, is the sudden re-invigoration of the legend and its impact on the writing of Australian history, a manifestation of what we have called the militarisation of Australian history. We have outlined the way in which government has promoted the celebration both of Anzac Day and the more general history of Australia's many and ongoing military engagements. Federal government departments and instrumentalities have been involved in unprecedented ways in the creation and dissemination of curriculum materials relating to war in a direct attempt to influence the content of classroom teaching. But we note, too, that the upsurge of interest in war has also swept the wider community. The replanting of memorial avenues of trees, the expansion and refurbishment of old and almost forgotten monuments and the building of new ones have resulted from near partnerships between the federal government, municipalities and local enthusiasts.

We have argued that while decaying monuments have been restored, antiquated rhetoric has also been called back into service and put to new uses. But the Anzac legend cannot be extracted from the ethos of the time of its birth and the attitudes and values that prevailed in 1915. It thus has become the vehicle by which the ideas of the Edwardian militarists are preserved and passed on to a new generation. At the centre of their creed was the conviction that war was the ultimate test for both nations and men. It was the beckoning threshold to individual heroism and national maturity. The central claim that Australia became a nation at Anzac Cove is the product of these ideas. Without that intellectual provenance the myth of Anzac would lose its great resonance as an event of transcendent national significance. The state-inspired encouragement for school children to admire and celebrate the heroism of the soldier would warm the hearts of the old Prussian militarists if they were ever to learn of it. The Anzac legend perpetuates an attitude to war in general and to World War 1 in particular. The belief that it was a source of unique and positive national virtue sails directly into the winds of contemporary global interpretations, which portray the conflict as the prime source of the brutalisation of the twentieth century that fuelled vast and terrible violence.

It is essential to look again at the overbearing idea that the spirit of the nation was born among the members of the Australian Imperial Force (AIF) on active service on the other side of the world. A significant problem with this proposition is the very uniqueness of their experience. The soldiers were far removed from normal life and its complex web of kinship, affections and responsibilities. They were in the distinctive situation of being in all male company for years on end and even then their associates were drawn from a very narrow male age cohort. We might well ask how such an unnatural society could give birth to a spirit of general relevance. Added to this is the fact that despite all the evidence of their anti-authoritarianism, the soldiers were governed by military laws which compelled obedience and severely punished mutiny or insubordination. They had to do as they were told and, even if grudgingly so, obey their senior officers. Their experience was far removed from the norms of civil society.

And then there is the inescapable matter of violence. It shadowed the experience of soldiers in a way unthinkable in ordinary life in Australia itself. The fear of cowardice was not unknown at home, but at the front it assumed compelling importance. The conflict at Gallipoli, in particular, was often conducted at close quarters, accompanied by vicious hand to hand fighting with direct, personal experience of killing. Respect, admiration and decoration accrued to those who could do it without flinching or even with dark, triumphant elation. But it is hard to prove that courage in the face of the enemy or close comradeship were distinctive characteristics of the Anzacs. Every army had its own brave, bold men, and the nature and outcome of the fighting were determined more by external factors like terrain, numbers, logistics and weaponry, rather than by national characteristics.

The interpretation of the Anzac spirit, offered in the governor-general's speech, would have surprised CEW Bean, the pre-eminent founder and celebrant of the legend. He did not suggest that it emerged on the Anzac Peninsula. Rather it was something that was born in the bush and carried into battle. It came from the experience of pioneering the country and above all from the resilience and toughness needed to settle the outback. Australian democracy, universal education and an open, meritocratic society shaped the specific quality of the diggers. The source of the spirit, according to Bean, was not to be found in military battle, but in the distinctive character of civilian life in the colonies. The diggers were citizen soldiers. Bean argued that they displayed these characteristics in the Middle East, but they did not create them there. More importantly they were noticed and admired by British commentators. Knowing very little about Australia itself, they thought they had discerned something new and distinctive in the behaviour and bearing of the soldiers. Their observations were treasured. Imperial praise mattered at the time to a degree that is hard for us to fully appreciate.

A further complication for the current apotheosis of the spirit of the Anzacs is that they were men of their time and therefore convinced white supremacists. They were the proud representatives of the White Australia Policy, which promoted racial purity at home and abroad. Indeed much of their self-confidence and élan came from their belief in their inherent superiority. They embodied it in their swagger, proud bearing and well-nourished physiques. Bean himself was a strong believer in the pre-eminence of what he thought of as the Anglo-Saxon race and the exploits of the soldiers confirmed for him that the ancient Teutonic spirit had not suffered by migration to the Antipodes.

The dark side of such racial cockiness was the contemptuous treatment of non-Europeans and in the Middle East, the Egyptians, Turks, Palestinians and Bedouin. The bush values of the Australian diggers included pride in being white men. Some of the Australians behaved like overbearing bullies in their dealings with the people whose countries they were occupying. Others expressed amused kindly condescension. It was perhaps inevitable that the young Australians would assume that the extreme poverty they witnessed for the first time was associated with racial difference. The British authorities found this pattern of behaviour particularly useful when they used the AIF to help put down the nationalist uprising in Egypt in 1919 after the end of hostilities. The accompanying atrocities have been largely forgotten or repressed,[1] which is not really surprising for how would we explain arrogant contempt for other people's nationalist aspirations in terms of the spirit we wish to associate with our national character? And how do we explain this to a world that still remembers the White Australia Policy and remains only half convinced of our much proclaimed recantations?

For many observers at the time, the victory in World War 1 was intimately associated with the preservation and perpetuation of White Australia. When he returned to Australia from Europe after the signing of the Treaty of Versailles, Prime Minister WM Hughes was greeted by members of the Fremantle branch of the Returned Sailors' and Soldiers' Imperial League of Australia (RSSILA) who congratulated him for his successful fight to keep Australia white. For Hughes that struggle had been central to his life's work. When he rose in the parliament to report on his role at Versailles he declared:

> White Australia is yours. You may do with it what you
> please; but at any rate, the soldiers have achieved the
> victory, and my colleagues and I have brought that principle
> back to you from the Conference.[2]

Hughes' sentiments would have been re-assuring to those diggers who had wondered whether White Australia should have been engaged in defending Black Egypt.

In explaining the historic return to Anzac in the last decade we have seen a relationship between the militarisation of Australian history and the controversy over Aboriginal history known as the 'History Wars'. The same political leaders who emphasise the importance of our military heritage have been demonstrably uncomfortable when asked to deal with the century-long conflict on the frontiers of settlement. Thus we show no embarrassment, indeed even feel pride, in our invasion of Turkey at the behest of the British, but great reluctance to acknowledge the British invasion of Australia. Many resist the idea that an invasion ever took place. And while we restore old monuments and construct new ones to commemorate military conflict overseas, there are still no official memorials to those who died on the frontier. The leadership of the Australian War Memorial stoutly resists any suggestion that they should give recognition to domestic warfare. Like their partners at the Department of Veterans' Affairs they seem to think they have fulfilled their responsibility by celebrating the contribution of Aboriginal and Islander servicemen abroad. New Zealand has always recognised the significance of Maori resistance in their national story. In the Anzac War Memorial Museum in Auckland there is a monument to the memory of all those who gave their lives during the New Zealand Wars of 1845–72. How long will it be before a similar monument is commissioned in Australia?

And what of the leaders of Aboriginal resistance? Though known to history they are not known to the general community and, as a corollary, not appreciated. Many Australians seem quite incapable of recognising them as patriots who were defending their homelands and their way of life against superior weapons and ever increasing numbers of Europeans. Heroism, it seems, is a quality best displayed overseas. Just like our artists, our warriors had to go abroad to achieve recognition. And while we go to great expense to find and recover the bodies of fallen servicemen wherever they are in the world, no official attempt has ever been made to find, mark and commemorate the sites where Aborigines were shot down by settlers, soldiers and police.

There is no doubt that many Australians found the public discussion of frontier violence deeply disturbing and adopted the pejorative term 'Black armband history' as a way of discrediting the new critical history. Former prime minister John Howard was among those who regretted the discovery that white Australia had a black history and it was central to his frequently voiced complaint that history was being used to make young people feel ashamed of their country.

It was time then to open up a new front in the History Wars. The vigorous official promotion of the history of Australian engagement in overseas wars was at one level a response to those histories that had complicated a once simple story of heroic explorers and noble, albeit tough, frontiersmen. The bushman overseas, glorified by Bean in the creation of the Anzac legend, outshone his stay-at-home cousins whose ancestors had dispossessed the Aborigines. Thus we show pride in our engagement in overseas wars as willing assistants to our great and powerful friends, while feeling embarrassment over the one war which was ours and ours alone, the long and sporadic conflict over the control of the continent and the exploitation of its resources.

The Anzac legend has also worked to normalise the deployment of Australian forces overseas and to deflect the critical observation that very few of the world's other small to middle sized powers have been so constantly engaged in conflict as Australia has been so far from its own borders. Engagement in foreign wars has been one of the most distinctive features of Australia's twentieth century history. Many of them have been what are now commonly called wars of choice rather than wars of necessity. The departure and return of expeditionary forces has been a recurring occasion for inflated political rhetoric with references to Anzac liberally and ritually employed to sanctify the operations in question. If latter day servicemen displayed the spirit of the Anzacs who could fault them or question the politicians who sent them away? As former Labor leader Kim Beazley noted at the launch of Craig Stockings's book *Bardia: Myth, Reality and the Heirs of Anzac*, politicians need the Anzac myth, or they would never be able to convince soldiers to go to war.

The cult of the warrior stands in the way of critical appraisal of Australian engagement in overseas wars. Many people feel constrained in criticising Australian involvement when our personnel are in the field and when they return, a clear-eyed assessment of the engagement is discouraged. Anti-Vietnam War protesters are, as we have seen, routinely disparaged. Admiration, not analysis, is what is now expected from historians. The recent return of the last troops to serve in Iraq was particularly instructive. Twenty thousand Australians had served in the country or its territorial waters. The engagement had lasted for six years. Reporting the return of the last contingent the local papers observed that it was a: 'Quiet end to a six year invasion.'[3]

There was indeed very little of the intense debate, once the troops were on the ground, about the wisdom or the morality of the war, of the sort that occurred in the United States, with a constant stream of critical, well informed books and articles. In Britain, concern about the war forced Prime Minister Gordon Brown to set up a high level committee to examine the reasons for the commitment and senior jurists seriously speculated as to whether Tony Blair should be charged with war crimes. But in

Australia there was just a quiet end to the six-year war.

There has been almost no serious discussion about how or why our country became involved in Iraq and there is very little serious analysis of the reason we currently have troops in Afghanistan and how long they will stay there. Indeed the present government has discouraged any serious assessment of what, if anything, Australia is likely to gain from either venture. There may be some retrospective evaluation of the Iraq War within the bureaucracy, but the public will presumably never hear about it. Nor do we know how much this military expedition cost the taxpayer. As Prime Minister Kevin Rudd told a radio journalist, while Labor hadn't agreed with the invasion of Iraq, he was not going to discuss it now because, 'serving troops should never be put in the middle of a political bunfight'.[4]

Why write a critical book about celebration of the Anzac spirit when so many people, from the governor-general down, treat it with reverence, and wonder if, as a nation, they can 'do it justice?' It is a fair question and a sensitive subject. The debate which followed the public lecture on the 'Myth of Anzac' in Melbourne, discussed in the introduction, showed what depth of feeling was invested in the Anzac story and the extent of some people's personal identification with it. We are aware of the upsurge of interest in the subject, we note the proliferation of war books and the popularity of pilgrimages to Gallipoli, the battlefields of France and the Kokoda track. But we also know that many Australians are deeply disturbed by and recoil from the militarisation of our history. And they feel that their concerns are overwhelmed by well funded, much publicised, official rhetoric. They are disturbed that criticism of the myth of Anzac is often seen as tantamount to disloyalty. With Australians positioned as either for or against the Anzacs, the digger has once again become a divisive figure as much as a unifying one.

Like the many Australians who are concerned with the homage paid to the Anzac spirit and associated militarisation of our history, we are concerned about the ways in which history is used to define our national heritage and national values. We suggest that Australians might look to alternative national traditions that gave pride of place to equality of opportunity and the pursuit of social justice: the idea of a living wage and sexual and racial equality. In the myth of Anzac, military achievements are exalted above civilian ones; events overseas are given priority over Australian developments; slow and patient nation-building is eclipsed by the bloody drama of battle; action is exalted above contemplation. The key premise of the Anzac legend is that nations and men are made in war. It is an idea that had currency a hundred years ago. Is it not now time for Australia to cast it aside?

NOTES

All websites in these endnotes were accessed on 27 October 2009.

Introduction: What have you done for your country?

1   The *Age* blog, 'Myth of Anzac', 23 April 2009. All following 'blog' quotes taken from this online discussion. See http://blogs.theage.com.au/yoursay/archives/2009/04/creation_of_a_n.html.
2   Quoted in KS Inglis, 'The Anzac tradition', *Meanjin*, 100th issue, vol 1, 1965, p 26.
3   RA Gollan, 'Nationalism, the labour movement and the Commonwealth' in G Greenwood (ed) *Australia: A Social and Political History*, Angus & Robertson, Sydney, 1967, p 146.
4   Anzac Day Commemoration Committee, 'The spirit of ANZAC', 2009, available at http://www.anzacday.org.au.
5   Prime Minister Howard's Australia Day speech, *Sydney Morning Herald*, 26 January 2006.
6   E Ashmead-Bartlett, 'Australians at the Dardanelles: Thrilling deeds of heroism', *Argus*, 8 May 1915. Quoted in D Gare and D Ritter (eds) *Making Australian History: Perspectives on the Past Since 1788*, Thomson, Melbourne, 2008, p 289.
7   E Foner, *The Story of American Freedom*, WW Norton and Co, New York, 1998, p xiii.
8   Editorial, *Age*, 27 April 2005.
9   JW Ward, 'Historiography' in AL McLeod (ed) *The Pattern of Australian Culture*, Oxford University Press, Melbourne, 1963.
10 Inglis, 'The Anzac tradition', p 34.
11 G Serle, 'The digger tradition and Australian nationalism', *Meanjin*, vol 2, 1965, p 149.
12 E Scott, *A Short History of Australia*, 5th ed, Humphrey Milford, Oxford University Press, Melbourne, 1928.
13 Scott, *A Short History of Australia*, p 348.
14 WK Hancock, *Australia*, Ernest Benn, London, 1930, p 63.
15 A Burke, 'The spirit of Anzac', available at http://www.anzacday.org.au.
16 Quoted in C Rasmussen, *Lesser Evil? Opposition to War and Fascism in Australia 1920-1941*, University of Melbourne, Melbourne, 1992, p 7.
17 Greenwood (ed) *Australia*, p v.
18 FK Crowley (ed) *A New History of Australia*, Heinemann, Melbourne, 1974, p 485.
19 Crowley (ed) *A New History of Australia*, pp 319–20.
20 Crowley (ed) *A New History of Australia*, p 320.
21 Crowley (ed) *A New History of Australia*, quoting GL Kristianson, *The Politics*

of *Patriotism: The Pressure Group Activities of the Returned Services League*, ANU Press, Canberra, 1966, p 361.

22 S Macintyre, *Oxford History of Australia*, Oxford University Press, Melbourne 1986, vol 4, p 177.

23 Macintyre, *Oxford History of Australia*, p 147.

24 M Dixson, *The Real Matilda: Women and Identity in Australia 1788 to the Present*, Penguin, Ringwood, 1976, p 12.

25 Hancock, *Australia*, p 66.

26 P Adam-Smith, *The Anzacs*, Nelson, Melbourne, 1978, p viii.

27 CMH Clark, *A History of Australia*, Melbourne University Press, Melbourne, 1981, pp 102–04.

28 Advertisement, *Mufti*, September/October 1980, p 7.

Chapter 1 Are nations really made in war?

1 Quoted in D Gare and D Ritter, *Making Australian History*, Thomson, Melbourne, 2008, p 311. My thanks to Marilyn Lake for this reference.

2 J Bourke, *An Intimate History of Killing*, Granta Books, London, 1999, p 1.

3 Quoted in LL Robson, *Australia and the Great War*, Macmillan, Melbourne, 1969, pp 46–7.

4 Quoted in JF Williams, *ANZACS, The Media and the Great War*, UNSW Press, Sydney, 1999, p 101.

5 Quoted in Williams, *ANZACS*, p 229.

6 Quoted in Williams, *ANZACS*, p 228.

7 Quoted in G Souter, *Lion and Kangaroo: Australia 1901-1919, The Rise of a Nation*, Collins, Sydney, 1976, p 229.

8 Quoted in Souter, *Lion and Kangaroo*, p 229.

9 Quoted in A Burke, *In Fear of Security*, Pluto, Sydney, 2004, p 35.

10 Quoted in G Seal, *Inventing Anzac: The Digger and National Mythology*, University of Queensland Press, Brisbane, 2004, p 35.

11 Quoted in M McKernan, *The Australian People and the Great War*, Nelson, Melbourne, 1980, p 18.

12 Quoted in Souter, *Lion and Kangaroo*, p 228.

13 TJ Lawrence, *The Principles of International Law*, 7th ed, Macmillan, London, 1929, p 219.

14 JA Cramb, *Germany and England*, John Murray, London, 1914, p 60.

15 JA Cramb, *The Origin and Destiny of Imperial Britain*, John Murray, London, 1915, pp 121, 125.

16 FN Maude, *War and the World's Life*, Smith Elder, London, 1907, p 5.

17 Quoted in P Crook, *Darwinism, War and History*, Cambridge University Press, Cambridge, 1994, p 80.

18 Quoted in T Tanner, *Compulsory Citizen Soldiers*, Alternative Publishing Co-operative, Sydney, 1960, p 90.

19 Quoted in JM Robertson, *Essays Towards Peace*, Watts, London, 1913, pp 26–7.

20 AL Gowan (ed) *H von Treitschke, Selections From His Lectures on Politics*, Gowan & Gray, London, 1914, pp 24, 39, 103–04.

21 RN Stromberg, *Redemption by War: The Intellectuals and 1914*, Regent's Press, Kansas, 1982, p 89.

22 J Keegan, *The First World War*, Hutchinson, London, 1998, p 456.

23 G Murray, *Thoughts on War*, Oxford University Press, London, 1914, p 4.

24 Quoted in C Playne, *The Neurosis of Nations*, Allen & Unwin, London, 1925, p 96.

25 Lawrence, *The Principles of International Law*, p 563.

26 P Laity, *The British Peace Movement*, Clarendon, Oxford, 2001, pp 180–82.

27 DS Jordan, *War and the Breed*, Beacon Press, Boston, 1915, preface.

28 JA Hobson, *The German Panic*, Cobden Club, London, 1913, p 22.

29 Hobson, *The German Panic*, p 37.

30 GP Gooch, *Imperialism in the Heart of Empire*, Fisher & Unwin, London, 1901, p 318.

31 HM Chittenden, *War and Peace*, McLurg, Chicago, 1911, pp 41–2.

32 LC Jane, *The Nations at War*, Dent, London, 1914, p 5.

33 N Angell, *The Great Illusion?*, Heinemann, London, 1914, p 280.

34 Jordan, *War and the Breed*, preface.

35 GB Shaw, preface to A Fenner Brockway, *Is Britain Blameless?*, National Labour Press, London, 1915.

36 *Sydney Morning Herald*, 16 August 1917.

37 Quoted in R Gerster, *Big-Noting: The Heroic Theme in Australian War Writing*, Melbourne University Press, Melbourne, 1987, p 36.

38 Gerster, *Big-Noting*, p 79.

39 Gerster, *Big-Noting*, p 118.

40 T Judt, 'What have we learned if anything?', *New York Review of Books*, 1 May 2008, p 18.

Chapter 2 Colonial Cassandras: Why weren't the warnings heeded?

1 WH Holborow: New South Wales, *Votes & Proceedings* (NSW V&P), 1885, p 179; J Robertson: NSW V&P, 1885, pp 107, 105.

2 EA Baker: NSW V&P, 1885, p 39.

3 J Fletcher: NSW V&P, 1885, pp 110–11.

4 AJ Gould: NSW V&P, 1885, p 25.

5 D Buchanan: NSW V&P, 1885, pp 99–100.

6 Fletcher: NSW V&P, 1885, p 197.

7 MJ Hammond: NSW V&P, 1885, p 193; A Cameron: NSW V&P, 1885, p 24.

8 J Buchanan: NSW V&P, 1885, pp 99–100.

9 C Connolly, 'Manufacturing "spontaneity": The Australian offers of troops for the Boer War', *Historical Studies*, vol 18, no 70, April 1978.

10 JRA Connolly: West Australia, *Parliamentary Debates* (WA PD), 1899, p 1560.

11 FCB Vosper and J Forrest: WA PD, 1899, p 1559.

12 E Barton: NSW V&P, 1899, pp 1459–56.

13 A Dawson: Queensland, *Parliamentary Debates* (Qld PD), 1899, p 344; H Turley: Qld PD, 1899, p 389.

14 JC Stewart: Qld PD, 1899, p 452.

15 W Kidston: Qld PD, 1899, p 416.

16 WA Robinson: South Australia, *Parliamentary Debates* (SA PD), 1899, p 148; EL Batchelor: SA PD, 1899, p 624.

17 T Price: SA PD, 1899, p 627.

18 HB Higgins: Victoria, *Parliamentary Debates* (Vic PD), 1899, p 1777.
19 Quoted in C Wilcox, *Australia's Boer War*, Oxford University Press, Melbourne, 2002, p 334.
20 Quoted in T Tanner, *Compulsory Citizen Soldiers*, Alternative Publishing Co-operative, Sydney, 1980, p 31.
21 Quoted in Tanner, *Compulsory Citizen Soldiers*, p 148.
22 Quoted in Tanner, *Compulsory Citizen Soldiers*, p 109.
23 DS Jordan, *The Days of a Man*, Harrap, London, 1922, vol 2, pp 213–14.
24 Committee of Imperial Defence Minutes, 83–119, p 34, National Archives (UK); Cabinet Papers, 2/2.
25 *Japan Times*, 26 August 1911.
26 Committee of Imperial Defence Minutes, 108, p 3; 110, p 3.
27 Hamilton papers, letter to Asquith, 14 April 1914, 5/1/87, King's College, London.
28 C Lucas, *Greater Britain and Greater Rome*, Clarendon Press, Oxford, 1912, pp 174–75.
29 ED Millen: Australia, *Parliamentary Debates* (Cth PD), 1914, p 99.
30 J Stewart: Cth PD, 1914, pp 97–8; Millen: Cth PD, 1914, p 129.
31 HB Higgins: Vic PD, 1899–1900, p 1798.
32 JA Hobson, *The Psychology of Jingoism*, Grant Richards, London, 1901, p 42.
33 R Pryor, *Gallipoli*, UNSW Press, Sydney, 2009, p xvi.
34 N Ferguson, *The Pity of War*, Basic Books, London, 1998, p 462.
35 J Keegan, *The First World War*, Hutchinson, London, 1998, p 3.

Chapter 3 Whatever happened to the anti-war movement?

1   Quoted in C Rasmussen, *The Lesser Evil? Opposition to War and Fascism in Australia 1920-1941*, University of Melbourne, Melbourne, 1992, p 10.
2   Quoted in Rasmussen, *The Lesser Evil?*, p 13.
3   D Rose, 'A History of Anti-War Organisations in Victoria, 1933–1939: A Study of the Movement Against War and Fascism, the Labor Anti-War Committee and the International Peace Campaign', MA thesis in History, La Trobe University, 1976, pp 3, 2. KS Inglis, 'Reluctant retreat from all-solemn observance', *Sydney Morning Herald*, 26 April 1964.
4   Rasmussen, *Lesser Evil?*, p 19.
5   Quoted in Rasmussen, *Lesser Evil?*, p 20.
6   M Lake, *The Limits of Hope: Soldier Settlement in Victoria, 1915-38*, Oxford University Press, Melbourne, 1987, pp 170, 197.
7   Lord Robert Cecil, 'The "Future of Civilization": Nobel Lecture' quoted in Rose, 'A History of Anti-War Organisations in Victoria, 1933–1939', p 17.
8   Rasmussen, *Lesser Evil?*, p 10.
9   Rasmussen, *Lesser Evil?*, p 10.
10 Rasmussen, *Lesser Evil?*, p 75.
11 Rasmussen, *Lesser Evil?*, p 88.
12 GL Kristianson, *The Politics of Patriotism: The Pressure Group Activities of the Returned Servicemen's League*, ANU Press, Canberra, 1966, p 103.
13 Quoted in P Sekuless and J Rees, *Lest We Forget: The History of the Returned Services League 1916-86*, Rigby, Sydney, 1986, p 1.

14 G Havers, 'Lest we forget?', *Honi Soit*, 24 April 1958.

15 Havers, 'Lest we forget'.

16 Havers, 'Lest we forget'.

17 *Sydney Morning Herald*, 6 May 1958; *Age*, 2 May 1960.

18 *Honi Soit*, 15 May 1958.

19 CW Joyce, 'Press too one-sided about Anzac Day', *Mufti*, 4 July 1959.

20 'The Anzac story', *Mufti*, 3 April 1961.

21 D Ferrero, 'The spirit of Anzac', *Honi Soit*, 21 April 1960.

22 D Ferrero, 'The spirit of Anzac' reprinted in *Farrago*, 29 April 1960; letter to editor, *Farrago*, 13 May 1960.

23 *Farrago*, 6, 13 May 1960; 3 May 1960.

24 Quoted in D Petersen, 'It's a dig at the old digger', *Sun*, 8 April 1961.

25 A Seymour, *The One Day of the Year* in *Three Australian Plays*, Penguin, Ringwood, 1963, p 27.

26 Seymour, *The One Day of the Year*, pp 80, 75.

27 A Seymour, 'An old warhorse returns to the fray', *Newswrite: Newsletter of the New South Wales Writers' Centre*, April 2003.

28 A Seymour, 'Letter to the editor', *Sydney Morning Herald*, 1 July 1961.

29 *Sydney Morning Herald*, 24 June 1961.

30 *Sydney Morning Herald*, 26 May 1965.

31 'Australian play is applauded', source and date unknown, press clippings Alan Seymour papers, MS 9198, National Library of Australia.

32 'Tokyo's One Day', *Bulletin*, 26 February 1966.

33 'If you are addressing a school', *Mufti*, 3 April 1961.

34 Quoted in B Buckley, 'A new hope for the RSL? More than booze and anti-Communism?', *Bulletin*, 23 April 1966.

35 *Oz*, 14 October 1964.

36 *Oz*, 14 October 1964.

37 KS Inglis, *Sacred Places: War Memorials in the Australian Landscape*, Melbourne University Press, Melbourne, 1998, p 379.

38 Inglis, 'Reluctant retreat from all-solemn observance', discussing the inter-war years.

39 W Crouch, 'Do we still need Anzac Day?', *Sydney Morning Herald*, 24 April 1974.

40 *Age*, 26 April 1969.

41 A Curthoys, '"Shut up you bourgeois bitch": Sexual identity and political action in the anti-Vietnam War movement' in J Damousi and M Lake (eds) *Gender and War: Australians at War in the Twentieth Century*, Cambridge University Press, Melbourne, 1995.

42 A Howe, 'Anzac mythology and the feminist challenge' in Damousi and Lake (eds) *Gender and War*, pp 304–05.

43 J McLeod, 'The fall and rise of Anzac Day: 1965 and 1990 compared', *War and Society*, vol 20, no 1, May 2002, p 150.

44 A Perkins, 'The new Anzacs', *Sun*, 27 April 1981.

45 A Seymour, *The One Day of the Year* (1985 revised version) in *Three Australian Plays*, Penguin, Ringwood, 1994, p 90.

46 Seymour, *The One Day of the Year* (1985 revised version), p 90.

47 Seymour, 'An old warhorse returns to the fray', p 7.

Chapter 4 Why do we get so emotional about Anzac?

1   AAP, 'Paul Keating is absolutely wrong about Gallipoli Anzac legend, Kevin Rudd says', *News.com.au*, 31 October 2008. My thanks to Mark McKenna for this and subsequent newspaper references.
2   Editorial, *Sydney Morning Herald*, 23–24 April 2005.
3   Editorial, *Age*, 25 April 2009.
4   See M McKenna and S Ward, '"It was really moving, mate": The Gallipoli pilgrimage and sentimental nationalism in Australia', *Australian Historical Studies*, vol 38, no 129, 2007, pp 141–51.
5   The transcript of John Howard's speech, Armistice Day 2004, can be found online at http://parlinfo.aph.gov.au.
6   RG Collingwood, *The Idea of History*, Clarendon Press, Oxford, 1946, p 304.
7   See for example the work of Carol and Peter Stearns in the United States: *Anger: The Struggle for Emotional Control in the United States*, University of Chicago Press, Chicago, 1986; C Kaplan, *Sea Changes: Essays on Culture and Feminism*, Verso, London, 1986; and P Stearns and J Lewis, *An Emotional History of the United States*, New York University Press, New York, 1998.
8   See BH Rosenwein, 'Worrying about emotions in history', *American Historical Review*, June 2002, p 837.
9   See *Labour of Loss: Mourning, Memory and Wartime Bereavement in Australia*, Cambridge University Press, Cambridge, 1999; *Living with the Aftermath: Trauma, Nostalgia and Grief in Post-war Australia*, Cambridge University Press, Cambridge, 2001; *Freud in the Antipodes: A Cultural History of Psychoanalysis*, UNSW Press, Sydney, 2005. On the political deployment of the language of loss see also M Lake, 'Citizenship as non-discrimination: Acceptance or assimilationism? Political logic and emotional investment in campaigns for Aboriginal rights in Australia, 1940–1970', *Gender and History Special Issue: Gender, Citizenships and Subjectivities*, vol 13, no 3, November 2001.
10 B Scates, *Returning to Gallipoli: Walking the Battlefields of the Great War*, Cambridge University Press, Melbourne, 2006.
11 KS Inglis, 'They shall not grow old', *Age*, 30 April 2005.
12 AF Davies, *Skills, Outlooks and Passions: A Psychoanalytic Contribution to the Study of Politics*, Cambridge University Press, Cambridge, 1980, p 344.
13 J Pearlman, 'Rudd promises to publicly honour Iraq troops', *Age*, 1 August 2009.
14 John Howard Anzac Day address, Canberra, 25 April 2003.

Chapter 5 Anzac Day: How did it become Australia's national day?

1   Board quoted in G Souter, *Lion and Kangaroo: Australia 1901-1919, The Rise of a Nation*, Collins, Sydney, 1976, p 229; also see J Beaumont, *The Anzac Legend: Australia's War 1914–1918*, pp 166–71 (Beaumont quotes Alistair Thompson on the Melbourne Shrine of Remembrance); also see report of Anzac Day in *Daily Telegraph*, 26 April 1938, p 1.
2   For Prime Minister Kevin Rudd's comments, see Editorial, *Age*, 25 April 2009.
3   KS Inglis, *Sacred Places: War Memorials in the Australian Landscape*, Melbourne University Publishing, Carlton, 2008 (first published 1998), p 572 and KS Inglis, 'They shall not grow old', *Age*, 30 April 2005.

4   V Wilcox in *Weekend Australian*, 25 April 1981.

5   Editorial, *Australian*, 23 April 1980, also see Editorial, *Australian*, 27 April 1981.

6   Editorial, *Sydney Morning Herald*, 31 December 1988; also see M McKenna, 'Metaphors of light and darkness: The politics of "Black Armband History"', *Melbourne Journal of Politics*, vol 25, 1998, pp 71–2.

7   Editorial, *Australian*, 23 April 1980, Editorial, *Australian*, 27 April 1981.

8   For examples of the queen's message on Anzac Day see *Canberra Times*, 25 April 1940 and *Canberra Times*, 26 April 1965, *Sydney Morning Herald*, 25 April 1959, p 1 and 25 April 1963, p 1; also see Queen Elizabeth II's Australia Day message, 1970.

9   T Stephens, *Sydney Morning Herald*, 26 April 1988; Bruce Ruxton's comments can be found in *Weekend Australian*, 26 April 1982, on Turks leading the march, see *Canberra Times*, 26 April 1974; on the history of the treatment of Vietnam veterans see M McKenna, 'Howard's warriors' in R Gaita (ed) *Why the War was Wrong*, Text, Melbourne, 2003, pp 167–200.

10 Editorial, *Sydney Morning Herald*, 26 April 1940; on 'bloodlust', see Editorial, *Sydney Morning Herald*, 26 April 1990; Bob Hawke's speech reported in both the *Australian* and the *Sydney Morning Herald*, 26 April 1990; also see Hawke's website   http://www.library.unisa.edu.au/bhpml/speeches_photos.asp,   which contains the full transcript of his speech; E Ashmead-Bartlett, 'Australians at the Dardanelles: Thrilling deeds of heroism', *Argus*, 8 May 1915 quoted in D Gare and D Ritter (eds) *Making Australian History: Perspectives on the Past Since 1788*, Thomson, Melbourne, 2008, p 289.

11 The full text of Hawke's Australia Day speech in 1988 can be found on his website, http://www.library.unisa.edu.au/bhpml/speeches_photos.asp.

12 Hawke in *Sydney Morning Herald*, 26 April 1990, pp 1, 4.

13 On Paul Keating see *Weekend Australian*, 24–25 April 1993, p 1 and editorial; also see the liftout in the *Australian*, 26 April 2000.

14 On John Howard and the flag, see *Australian*, 25 April 1996, p 1 and editorial, also on the same day, see Donald Horne's op ed, in which he argued that that young Australians were looking for some articulation of binding values in Anzac Day and in Australia Day.

15 *Australian*, 25 and 26 April 2000, the paper's editorial on 25 April noted the 'pride' of the pilgrims; Howard at the Dawn Service Gallipoli 25 April 2000, reported in *Sydney Morning Herald*, 26 April 2000; also see Howard's interview with Mike Munro, *A Current Affair*, 26 April 2000, both this interview, and the full transcript of Howard's speech at Gallipoli, were drawn from Howard's website when he was prime minister (not currently available).

16 For details on Howard's encouragement of Anzac Day, particularly the international context of war, see M McKenna, 'The Anzac myth' in T Jones (ed) *The Best Australian Political Writing*, Melbourne University Press, Melbourne, 2008, pp 333–35; also see M McKenna and S Ward, '"It was very moving Mate" Anzac Day and sentimental nationalism', *Australian Historical Studies*, no 129, April 2007, pp 141–51.

17 See Howard's Anzac Day addresses, 25 April 2001, especially 25 April 2003 and 25 April 2005; also Howard at the State funeral for Alec Campbell (the last Anzac Gallipoli veteran), 24 May 2002, and Howard nominating Anzac Cove to

head a new National Heritage List, Editorial, *Age*, 27 April 2005; also Howard's Australia Day speech as reported in the *Sydney Morning Herald*, 26 January 2006, p 11, in which he proclaimed: 'we should have faith in what we have achieved and what we have become ... the time has come for a root and branch renewal of the teaching of Australian history in our schools'; for examples of press support for the new Anzac Day see Editorial, *Sydney Morning Herald*, 23–24 April 2005, p 30 and Editorial, *Australian*, 19 October 2005 and Editorial, *Australian*, 25 April 2000 noting the 'pride' of the pilgrims and P Kelly, 'Empire's battle was our fight too', *Australian*, 26 April 2000, in which Kelly wrote: 'The Gallipoli resurgence enshrines Anzac as the central and unifying story of Australia's national spirit.' The Labor Opposition, led by Kim Beazley, was not far behind, see Beazley in Australia, *Parliamentary Debates*, House of Representatives, 17 June 2002, p 3414, Anzac Day, Beazley told the House, was now the 'core element of our national psychology'; finally see Howard's Australia Day address in 2007, reported in all major broadsheets the following day.

18 Howard speaking at Australia House, 10 November 2003 ('Australians at War'), also see Howard visiting Iraq in 2005, where he addressed Australian troops at Camp Smitty, Al Muthanna Province, 25 July 2005: 'we have never had a war-like military tradition we Australians, we only deploy military force in a right and a just cause'; Vox pops from ABC AM, 25 April 2005 and *Age*, 25 April 2005; for the beer-soaked celebrations of the so called pilgrims to Anzac Cove, see A Gilbertson, 'In the fields of the fallen', *Sydney Morning Herald*, Good Weekend, 23 April 2005, pp 28–30.

19 Howard equated history with 'national inheritance', in his *Quadrant* address, 3 October 2006; for Howard's history of pride and honour see his Anzac Day address, 25 April 2001.

20 *Today*, 25 April 2006; ABC TV, *The First Tuesday Book Club*, 24 April 2007; G Henderson in *Sydney Morning Herald*, 19 April 2005; my thanks to Mads Clausen and Stuart Ward for these references.

21 *Sydney Morning Herald*, 26 April 1965, p 2; for examples of fears that Anzac Day would die with the diggers, see *Australian*, 25 April 1969 and 26 April 1973, also Editorial, *Courier Mail*, 26 April 1973, p 1; for clashes see *West Australian*, 26 April 1969 and 24 April 1972, also *Courier Mail*, 26 April 1968; for the throwing of red paint, see P Cochrane, *Australians at War*, ABC Books, Sydney, 2001, p 219; for examples of welcome-home parades for Vietnam veterans see *Courier Mail*, 13 November 1970, p 3 and *Age*, 26 April 1972.

22 Editorial, *Sydney Morning Herald*, 25 April 1967; *West Australian*, 24 April 1965; on new nationalism, see Editorial, *Australian*, 25 April 1973; on the controversy over the playing of 'Advance Australia Fair' on Anzac Day see *Sydney Morning Herald*, 26 April 1974, *Courier Mail*, 26 April 1974, *Age*, 26 April 1974; on the lack of agreement over a new national identity, see Editorial, *Australian*, 25 April 1969 and Editorial, *Australian*, 25 April 1967; for examples of press support for Anzac Day as Australia's only true national day, see Editorial, *Sydney Morning Herald*, 25 April 1970 and 25 April 1972, also *Courier Mail*, 25 April 1970; my thanks to Stuart Ward for all newspaper references from the 1960s–80s used in this essay.

Chapter 6 How do schoolchildren learn about the spirit of Anzac?

1   Unless otherwise stated all the information about the Department of Veterans' Affairs (DVA) programmes and funding can be found in DVA annual reports and on its website http://www.dva.gov.au.

2   M Caulfield, *Voices of War: Stories from the Australians at War Film Archive*, Hodder, Sydney, 2006. See also *Gallipoli: The First Day* (the full 3D interactive site), available at http://www.abc.net.au/innovation/gallipoli.

3   Prime Minister John Howard, *Quadrant* address, 3 October 2006.

4   A Clark, *History's Children: History Wars in the Classroom*, UNSW Press, Sydney, 2008, p 46.

5   K Windschuttle, *The Fabrication of Aboriginal History*, Macleay Press, Sydney, 2002; R Manne (ed) *Whitewash: On Keith Windschuttle's Fabrication of Aboriginal History*, Black Inc Agenda, Melbourne, 2003.

6   L Reed, *Bigger Than Gallipoli: War, History and Memory in Australia*, UWA Press, Nedlands, pp 14–15.

7   DVA, *Annual Report 1996-97*.

8   DVA, *Annual Report 1999–2000*, pp 84–5; P Bowers, *Anzacs, The Pain and the Glory of Gallipoli*, Australia Post, Melbourne, 1999.

9   DVA, *Annual Report 1999–2000*, p 85.

10 DVA, *Annual Report 2001–02*.

11 DVA, *Annual Report 2001–02*.

12 DVA, *Annual Report 2002–03*.

13 DVA, *Annual Report 2002–03*.

14 DVA, *Annual Report 2004-05*.

15 See the websites: http://www.anzacsite.gov.au and http://www.ww2australia.gov.au.

16 Clark, *History's Children*, p 47.

17 Clark, *History's Children*, pp 46–7.

Epilogue: Moving on?

1   S Brugger, *Australians and Egypt*, Melbourne University Press, Melbourne, 1980.

2   Australia, *Parliamentary Debates*, vol lxxxix, 1919, p 12175. See M Lake and H Reynolds, *Drawing the Global Colour Line: White Men's Countries and the Question of Racial Equality*, Melbourne University Press, Melbourne, 2008, pp 308–09.

3   *Mercury* (Hobart), 1 August 2009.

4   *Mercury* (Hobart), 1 August 2009.

Index